Tim Herzberg

A Quart' more, please?

My three month adventure with the

Bioness NESS L300

Manufactured and published by

BoD – Books on Demand

Norderstedt

Cover: Image of a human body in a pentagram, Heinrich Cornelius Agrippa von Nettesheim, (Public domain)

ISBN: 9783746095424

First edition

Thanks.

(just like that)

Diagnosis

Severe atypical ICB (intracerebral bleed) rt. cen. (10/2009)

near micro-AVM (arteriovenose Malformation) rt. cen.

with surgical resection (11/2009).

Symptomatic Epilepsy, lt. hemiparesis.

For more check my first book:

 "Halftime: Experiences of a neuro", ISBN-13: 978-3732287000

Manufactured and published byISBN: 3732236072

Preface

The NESS L300 Foot Drop system helps lift a drop-foot and counters an inward rotation by timed electro stimulation to accomplish a more natural gait. It does this through a charge dispensing cuff that is strapped around the calf below the knee. In combination with a pressure sensor, which can be integrated into the shoe, the impulse is timed so that the appropriate muscles contract at exactly the right moment.

Heußweg
Heu
Edeka
Emilienstraße
Eichenstraße
Im Gehölz
Im Geh
Ring 2
B 5
Karstadt
Osterstraße
Henriettenstraße
Manna
Bio
Eicher
Karstadt
Eimsbüttel
Henriettenstraße
Osterstraße
Schulweg
Professor-
Reinmüller-
Platz 2
Osterstraße
Grundschule
Tornquiststraße
Henriettenstraße
Tornquiststraße
ofessor-
inmüller-
Platz
Schulweg
Tornquiststraße
Emilienstraße
Henriettenweg
Schulweg
Tegetth

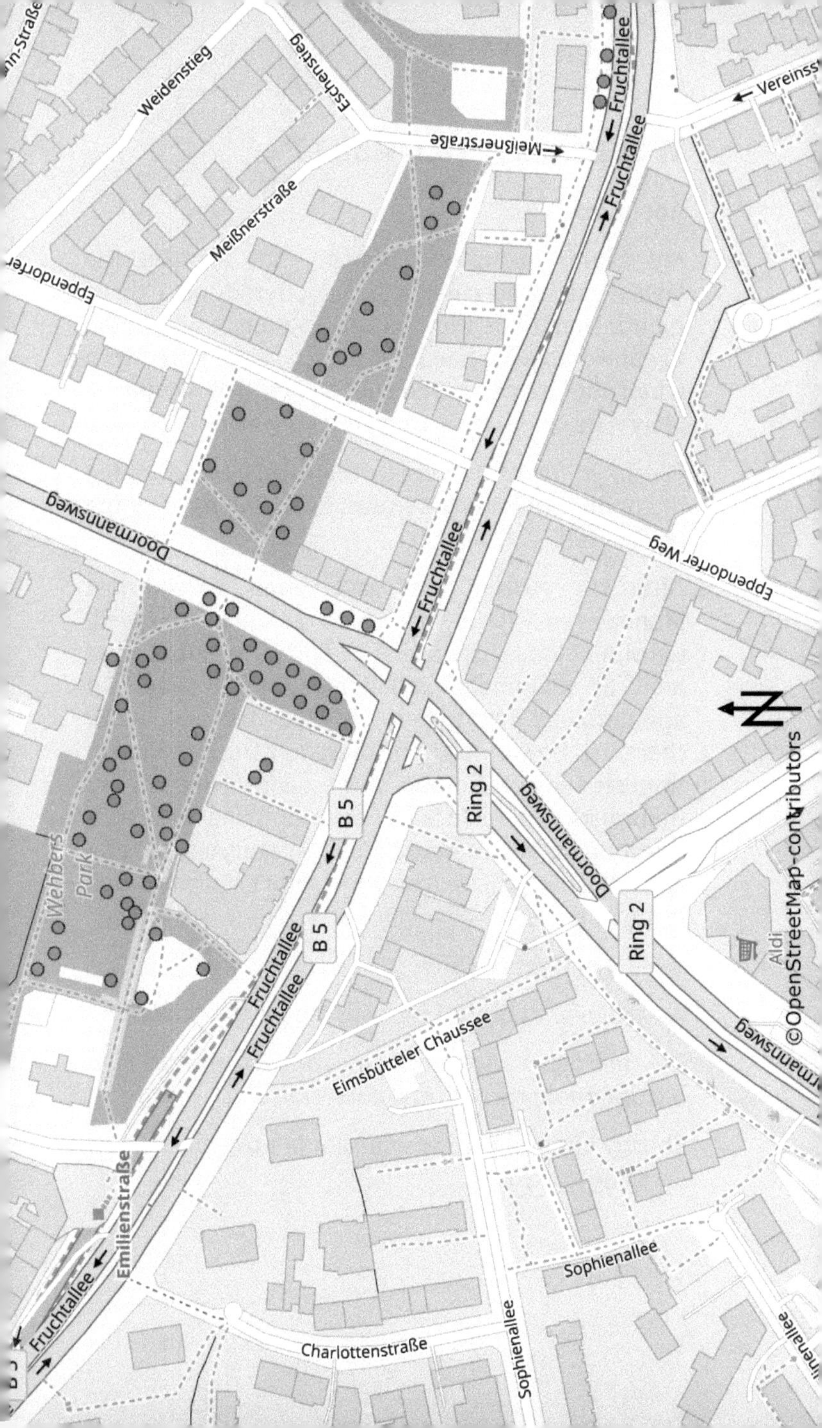

Weidenstieg
Eschenstieg
Meißnerstraße
Meißnerstraße
Eppendorfer
Doormannsweg
Fruchtallee
Fruchtallee
Fruchtallee
Vereinss
Eppendorfer Weg
N
© OpenStreetMap-contributors
Ring 2
Doormannsweg
Ring 2
Doormannsweg
Aldi
B 5
B 5
B 5
Wehbers Park
Fruchtallee
Fruchtallee
Emilienstraße
Fruchtallee
Fruchtallee
Eimsbütteler Chaussee
Sophienallee
Sophienallee
Charlottenstraße

Wednesday, 12.04.2017

About time!

My health insurance company has avoided the lawsuit at social court and has offered me a three month trial of the Bioness L300 system. I was in the deepfreeze department of a local wholesale store when the lawyer called me, asking if it would be okay if he could agree to that in my name.

"Yeah, go for it! As long as that doesn't undermine or conflict with any long-term provisioning after the trial. Sure!"

After the written cost assumption arrived last Monday, everything happened at amazing speed. Carolin (Bioness specialist at MPM, my supplier of medical equipment) called me and we made an appointment for today. I called Jan my work therapist. He wanted to be there too. Once again, I'm the test subject. No one in the near vicinity of my therapists and doctors has been supplied with such a system for such a long period. So everyone's really excited. That's the reason why I didn't sleep too well last night.

9 AM. I'm right on time.

As a regular at MPM, I wave to the receptionists.

"Hi, me again. Appointment with Carolin at nine o'clock, room three?" And go upstairs.

Shortly after, Jan arrives Carolin not too much later, carrying two cases.

"Oh my." I think. "How am I going to carry all that?"

But only the small one is for me. The big one holds the programming unit (which, sadly, I don't get. Yes, I'm a nerd) The Bioness L300 doesn't look as spectacular in real life as it does on the marketing material I've seen. But in this case, understatement is a good thing. I like it sleek. The L300 consists of the stimulation cuff, the gait sensor (which is placed between the soles of your shoe) and the small remote that controls the cuff.

"Drop your pants, time to try it on."

That's easier than expected, even one-handed. There's an indentation in the cuff, which goes under your kneecap so you know where the front is and so you don't wear it upside down. The cuff fits loosely unfastened, but it doesn't fall off, giving you enough time to grab behind your calf, find and grab the strap, bring it round to the front and snap it over the battery pack. Adjust the strap tight - but not too tight - so it doesn't constrict blood circulation. And that's it; easy as pie. But wait - first you have to wet the electrode pads.

After being added into the patient database of the programming unit and initialising a few basic settings, the cuff is switched on. A weird buzz pierces my calf. My foot instantly raised and turned to the left almost into a straight forward position. Carolin tapped a few times with the Stylus on the touchscreen of the programming unit and my foot twisted a little more until it was in a normal position. That was the end of my foot's inward rotation. After that we tested the strength of the stimulation against the foot drop. From painful to not perceptible, Carolin chose a setting that wasn't painful but gave maximum lift.

"Pants back up! Test walk!"

With my walking stick - a Nordic-walking stick that keeps me more upright, improving my overall posture (I also have a very stylish "old Fritz" - a cane with sterling silver head and ebony shaft that my therapists immediately forbade me to use because it was way too low and made me stoop. What a waste! But probably better that way) - I walk up and down the hallway a couple of times. A little unsteady at first, but that feeling recedes quickly. It feels as if my left foot glides over the carpet; or hovering! It's difficult to explain, and I'm not sure that describes it adequately. The stiff and heavy muscles and bones that define my left leg are back working for the first time in years. With each step my heel is the first part of my foot that touches the floor and I actually roll along the complete foot and finish with my toes. Unbelievable! I had hoped for some progress but had in no way expected that much. I try to relieve myself of my stick completely but ... Woahhh, that doesn't work all too well.

"Not yet," I think, "maybe later." One step at a time. Years and years of therapy with only gradual improvements have hammered patience into me.

Carolin explains the remote to me; shows me there's a training mode that can mobilise my ankle, keep the sinews flexible and the muscles supple.

She shows me how I can change the intensity of the electrostimulation (ES). The remote starts at 5 which corresponds to the standard setting Carolin determined for me, but I can increase the power to 9 or lower it to 0(zero). The rechargeable batteries need about four hours from flat to full - so easiest to recharge overnight. I get two felt electrodes that I should use alternately, changing them on a daily basis. The small case only just barely fits upright in my bag, and I (on a hunch) had already taken the biggest one I had. We agree to meet every now and then if needed, on Wednesdays at 9 AM at work therapy which is right next door to MPM.

And that's it. Done. I can go. Mine, for three months!

My initial impression while using the Bioness is that I'm very unsteady, probably because it's so unfamiliar - and the cuff's buzz is pretty distracting - but the biggest difference is that after seven years of absence, my leg is somewhat back in action. With a big grin on my face, it's off to work.

First thing I did at work was play with the training mode. I wore it until about three pm and it was time for my siesta. After my rest, the soles of my feet were so sensitive that I couldn't stand on them, so much so, I had to put shoes on to get to the toilet. But then again I hadn't really expected to get away with no side effects. To counter the expected muscle ache I swallowed a huge dose of magnesium.

Thursday, 13.04.

This morning I did have some muscle ache, but not as bad as expected. Today I'll try to keep it on all day. I may have to buy looser cut jeans; the cuff barely fits under my Levis 527s. The sore soles haven't returned. My physiotherapists are very enthusiastic and are looking into how to adjust my therapy to boost the positive effects of the system. In the meantime, they will take care of the side effects and mobilise my foot, ankle and hip. But it's still early and we can react in a flexible manner, adapting to problems or needs as they may arise.

I show them the difference, one walk with the system off and another with it on. First obvious, visible changes: faster, longer steps, and the inward rotation is gone. I now step down on the heel and roll off over the whole foot. That's probably the reason for my sole problems yesterday. I hadn't put any notable weight on my heel for years, because I usually step with my foot flat to the floor.

There is also a notable after-effect. Even after switching the system off there's still a distinct improvement in my gait pattern, but that effect wears off quickly.

One of my therapists noted that I seemed to lift my leg less using my hip, but he wasn't too sure. Usually, I lift my left leg by tipping my hip to the right because I have difficulty bending my knee. I told them that there was a huge improvement in my balance too. I assume that's because my left side is now definitely forced back into awareness.

And then I almost fried my therapist Artour. He tried on the cuff and then started training mode after I accidentally raised the level to 9. "Ooops, sorry 'bout that!" He jumped and screamed from pain. I've tried 9 on myself too and, yes it is very unpleasant, but it's not that painful. Then again, I do have a sensibility disorder; the ability to feel anything touching my left side is reduced to about 20%. Side effect: only a fifth of the pain actually reaches my brain.

When walking I hardly notice the ES at all. It just blends into my stride perfectly; giving the impulse at just the right time when the muscle should normally contract. The gait sensor in my shoe gives the order to buzz when weight is reduced on my left heel, lifting the foot at just the right moment. That all happens when I walk - and that's fine - however, while standing you unconsciously displace your weight from left to right all the time as a normal part of keeping your balance. Due to my disorders and lack of balance, I do this more than usual and every time I do, I get zapped! The first time I was so surprised I almost fell over. Switching the whole system off for such short time span is not an option - so I'll have to develop a workaround sometime soon. Today I dispensed static charges. It seems I'm all charged up. Off to Dithmarschen, my former homeland. It's family time. It's Easter.

Friday, 14.04.

Today: fair amount of muscle ache; a pause in my regimen? Almost. Squeezed in 20 minutes of training.

Saturday, 15.04.

I started today with 20 mins of training, then 60 metres of cobblestone with a strong headwind in Meldorf. We made a spontaneous trip to an optometrist because my glasses sit somewhat askew on my nose. I might order a new pair. And because of the spontaneity of the whole thing of course I didn't have my dioptre values on me; I had to have my eyes measured, again. We were about halfway through the test when the optician looked a little puzzled at me and says:

"Wait a second; I have to test a hunch ... "

His device goes clickety-clack, and a red circle appears in the middle of my right eye's field of view.

"Is the green cross in the middle of the red circle?" Green cross? Oh OK, up there, way up left. No, not even close."He cranks some wheels a couple of times: crank, crank, crank. The green cross shifts a little to the right and comes down a notch.

"Better?"

"A little, but still way off." I say. And then, I get it. A double vision test? I had double vision way back, but it went away again.

Crank, crank, crank, crank, crank, crank. Still closer, but cross and circle are still far apart. They're not even touching.

"That's it. It doesn't go any further." He says.

"Don't worry." I reply. "Doesn't bother me much in daily life." Surprise, surprise: My double vision is still there. "Glad to hear that. And your blind spot doesn't either?" (I'd told him about the missing lower left quadrant in my field of view.) "You only messed up two of the letter lines, and corrected yourself almost immediately."

"Yes but, it takes more work than the double images. I still have to do an active scan of the left lower area to see if I've missed anything. Funny thing is that it's not the eye that's impaired. I can't process the lower left of whatever I'm looking at. Doesn't matter if it's a page or picture, screen or face. The lower left just doesn't compute. All I can do is scan the missing area and hope that I find everything. Often enough something slips past me. It seems as if the part of my brain that's generally responsible for lower left is damaged. You see, my eyes haven't changed at all. And I had close to perfect sight before my brain haemorrhage. Nobody, neither neurologists nor neurosurgeons, not ophthalmologists, nor eye specialists and the like, has been able to give me a plausible explanation to why glasses now help my sight."

"Nor will they. That's because they just don't know. Nobody does. We are just beginning to understand the neurological aspects of sight. Most of the hardware issues are understood, but we've got a long way to go on the software."

"But it must be very exhausting to put the two images together all the time. It's not like it's only a little bit. In your case it's a huge discrepancy between the two, in fact, there is no prism film that's strong enough to help in your case."

"Well, after a long morning of screen-work I do tend to have difficulty concentrating and my overall cognitive capacity is notably reduced. Do you think that's the reason why?"

"I can't answer that, I'm not an expert, but it sounds like it's probably a factor."

"So, easy way out: wear glasses?" I ask.

"Seems so, but worse things can happen." He replies.

Yeah, I know, I've been there.

But I digress; back to the Bioness.

The ES was somewhat unpleasant today so I reduced the intensity first to 4 and then down to 3. Far more pleasant and I didn't notice any change in my gait.

Sometimes after an intensive Theratrainer session my ankles get irritated (my Theratrainer is like a cycle ergometer, only that mine has a built-in motor. You strap your feet onto the pedals switch it on and it mobilises your legs for you. Great device, and it's done a lot to keep me up on my legs.) After walking with the system for a few days my left ankle is occasionally irritated, but after a siesta it comes good. However, my quadriceps is doing overtime (the quadriceps - or quad - is the large muscle group on the front of your thigh that spans from your knee to your hip). My quad does that every now and then, even without new stimuli. It's a regular problem that I'm used to and which will now, become worse (at least in the initial stages) .

Sunday, 16.04.

Twenty minutes training today. Quad still hard but only irritated. Off to Süderbrarup - an unannounced visit to my Aunt and Uncle. Walked another 20 metres, had a few close calls because of the strong wind.

On my way back to Hamburg, whilst sitting almost horizontally, the cuff started to constrict the blood flow to my lower leg. I took it off and after three minutes of painful pins-and-needles in my foot everything was back to normal.

For the rest of the day I put on my wrist and hand orthosis, which was easier than expected. I thought the ES would affect my left hand more, but putting it on was no more difficult than it always was. My orthosis stops my fingers from clenching, which happens when I'm exposed to any type of stress, physical or mental. When stressed it is difficult, sometimes even impossible to put the Orthosis on. My expectation was that the ES would have had more impact.

Easter Monday, 17.04.

Upon waking, the ball of my left foot hurt. I was already wondering when this was going to happen. I believe everyone has a right to their 15 minutes of fame (in this case it was my left foot's time to shine), so I was not disappointed when I put my feet to the floor this morning. As long as it's only 15 minutes: fine by me. At least the muscle ache has gone away completely.

It's freezing outside today. A nasty north-easterly blowing straight out of Scandinavia slashes through town. That's why I only do half an hour of training mode. I didn't leave the flat today but I did cook a bunch of preserves. The Bioness system isn't made for the short distances whilst cooking in the kitchen - too many false impulses - so I switched it off. It seems to be a gadget for long distances.

I also seem to have soaked the electrodes. My skin underneath was extremely sodden. Tomorrow I should probably check that the pads are just moist, not dripping wet and wring them properly before putting the cuff on. You learn by experience.

Tuesday, 18.04.

Easter's done for another year. Welcome back to normal everyday life. It's much easier to evaluate the Bioness when on a consistent routine. First, a couple of laps via Ella, our company's controller. I had a couple of issues with my pension fund that needed her attention. Four times: 15 metres without my stick.

I get the impression that my balance is getting better and better. I'm also impeding the false ES impulses by keeping my full weight on my left heel, which is also good training because it further improves the awareness of my left leg. Sometimes I just love this technical jargon: good sensomotoric training. Or even better: suitably appropriated proprioceptive neuromuscular stimulation. It's going to take some time before that becomes an automatism. And it's not too high on the to-do-list because I have so many things that are more important to tackle than working on my ability to reel off tongue-twisting medical nomenclature.

I'm also getting used to the buzz from the unit more and more. It doesn't distract me half as much as it did a couple of days ago. Maybe it won't be a problem for too long. I just learned from the Bioness homepage that it's actually called functional electro-stimulation (FES).

Wednesday, 19.04.

Only 10 minutes training to accompany my espresso today – don't want to overdo it as who knows what my work therapist has come up with?

We walked halfway around the building and filmed my gait so we can prove that there's improvement when using the system. And there are things that have already improved. Most notable is the improved perception of my left side, meaning I can now put more weight on my left leg, making me more upright instead of constantly tilting to the right.

Other measures: shorten my stick by two inches; stroll 100 metres along Schulweg. Important: choose conditions so we get a uniform measurability and, if possible, remove any disruptive factors. And record as much as I can so that I can substantiate the need to my health insurance.

Things to keep in mind whilst walking: keep the stick close to my body (shortening the stick makes that easier) and walk with what I call my sailor's-gait (left leg: long step, far to the left; right leg: short step to the right. Lower my centre of gravity by trying to bend my knees slightly; push my left hip forward to correct my hip misalignment; exaggerate as needed. Warning: may look silly.

Oh, and don't fiddle with your medication! On days where my base muscle tone is high I like to take a higher dose of muscle relaxant. No more. All dosages are now fixed. Ten minutes of training is all I need. My left side is already (over-) loaded enough with the Bioness. That training combined with the 100 metre stroll should be sufficient. I've already installed a running app on my iPhone and I've measured the distance in Google Maps. From the corner of Henriettenstrasse to the third street lamp down Schulweg is 50 metres. There and back equals 100.

And he's off! It went well, almost too easy. It seems I underestimated the distance in the house, so it was more like 120 metres. Still, it was way too easy. But we're just starting - and it's more about quality than quantity. Consistency, not distance. I'll do that daily now for at least a week. I might increase the distance to 200 metres, which would be to the corner of Tornquiststrasse. Definitely feasible. It seems as if the Bioness allows me to walk longer and farther. Wouldn't that be great? I'll take that any day.

Thursday, 20.04.

No training this morning. I'm on my way to the district office to pick up my new passport - and there's lots of walking involved with that. Walked the "Sailor" all the way and did get a couple of weird looks. The app reported 110 metres in all. After work I even walked to the third street lamp in nice weather. So 200 metres overall. The 100 target is way too short. But I'll discuss that with Jan tomorrow.

Friday, 21.04.

This morning I have an appointment with my neurologist. Can't wait to hear what she says - after all, she's the one who prescribed me the system. I rolled up the leg of my pants and then put on the cuff so it's easier to show. But, it's very cold with a naked calf so I rolled it back down over the cuff with some difficulty.

She was very surprised by the very apparent, instant improvements. She noted that the inward rotation was almost completely gone, my gait had improved considerably and that I don't lift my leg off the floor with my hip as much. All that in only two weeks!

Back home, the weather betrayed me and forced me indoors with a nasty drizzle. So instead I took down the trash with the Bioness switched on. Because I need my good hand to carry the rubbish bag I can't use my stick, (sadly there's no GPS underground so I couldn't track the distance and because I couldn't use my stick, this walk wasn't going to be representative anyway). It was interesting to walk with the Bioness on and without a stick. Not as dangerous as the first time at MPM, but still a long way from doing it outside.

One of the electrodes is starting to smell a little. No wonder, always warm and moist with continuous skin contact. It was bound to happen. So I soaked today's with Sterilium. I expect it to cope with that. The entire seams look mechanically joined and not glued. I think Sterilium could dissolve glues of all sorts.

Saturday, 22.04.

The electrode smells way better. Thought so. Bad smells are commonly caused by bacteria and a little sterilisation helped. I'm not going to try cooking them. Yet.

This morning the sun peeks through the clouds every now and then and it's staying dry, so after my espresso I start. I walk to the third streetlamp; then past it; then all the way to Tornquiststrasse. The 200 metre mark was approved by Jan yesterday - as long as I'm consistent. Measurability!

Apropos measuring: I uninstalled the running app. It worked fine for three days, but then it tried to force me to register apparently "needing" personal information I wasn't going to provide. I didn't even bother reading the privacy guidelines. Instead I just picked a different GPS tracking app. They're a dime a dozen out there.

There's a nasty wind outside and the ground is wet. I check my rain app; there's no precipitation within a radius of 5 kilometres. So, I'm off. 200 metres! I concentrate on keeping my stick close to my body and pushing my hip forward and ... oops ... already back? How time perception alters when your mind is wandering somewhere else (or intensely focused on the job at hand). I managed the distance in 11:20. Is that good? Time will tell. At least it's a reference; something to build on.

Sunday, 23.04.

Heavy rain today, but every now and then there's a gap in the clouds and the sun peeks out. It's supposed to get better in the afternoon, so instead of a walk: Lunchtime! After feeding time - at about two o'clock - the sun's out for a short time. So I'm off! Outside, I get blasted by an icy wind, but I walk to the corner of Tornquiststrasse.

Along Schulweg it's somewhat sheltered from the wind (I live in a continental west wind zone and my track is on a north-south axis, so it's at right angles to the predominant winds). When I get to Tornquiststrasse I get caught in shower of soft hail. Good that I'm wearing a wide brimmed hat. I heard some years ago that you lose a large percentage of your body heat through your head. Since then I cover my head. Trilbys, docker caps, porkpies, travellers, fedoras, even a bowler. I've got quite a collection. But I don't wear baseball caps or cowboy hats. A ten-gallon Stetson looks silly in a city like Hamburg and I don't like the style anyway. One that's missing in my collection, and believe me I've tried really hard to get my hands on, is the original Jacques Cousteau red beanie.

The shower was gone in a minute and I was back on track. Time: 09:01. Wow! I was two whole minutes faster? Did I hasten because of the hail?

Back home, I find out that my GPS is only accurate to about 30 metres and only updates every 30 seconds. The map even shows that I jumped Schulweg several times today. I wouldn't even cross those four lanes at four in the morning let alone at rush hour. I may be brain damaged, but that doesn't mean I'm stupid.

But the time is accurate. I started and stopped at exactly the same place yesterday and today. So it really was two minutes faster. If I keep up this rate of improvement, I'll be breaking fundamental physics by the end of next week. But I expect that inertia and light speed won't allow that. Photons do have a rather large weight advantage on me.

Noteworthy: No notable muscle ache and my quadricep is almost quiet.

Monday, 24.04.

I wanted to walk directly after coming home, but the wind was even colder and I am definitely not attired warmly enough. It also feels as if the electrodes aren't moist enough and the FES isn't passed on to my muscles properly. That's why I move my siesta to the top of my agenda. Afterwards, it's drizzling and the wind has picked up, but now I can clothe myself appropriately.

I change electrodes and moisten the new one properly, (Buzz...) grab a coat and wide brimmed hat and go outside. I make good speed on the way to the corner. About two thirds of the way back, my quadriceps cramps and I'm forced to pause awhile. The rest of the way home isn't too far. I complete it, lean my stick against the wall and stop the tracker. I'm faster again: 08:28 - that's great! A pity that my quad differs in that opinion, because he's gone crazy - muscle tone hard as concrete and I even had a light tremor - haven't had that in ages. So it's more magnesium today. I refrain from taking more muscle relaxant.

Tuesday, 25.04.

It's pouring, plus the rain app shows massive lightning strikes in northern Hamburg, so I take my hand orthosis with me (just because I can't walk doesn't' mean there's nothing else I can do). My quad has tempered down, it's still a little pressure sensitive, but that's nothing new.

On my way to Physiotherapy there's one last heavy shower and that's it. The clouds dissipate and the sun bursts out. Artour kneads my quad back into form, mobilises my left arm and shoulder.

Back home; a quick strengthening double espresso and off into the fray. Sadly, in my morning's absence, two new construction sites have been set up on my track. But I can switch to the bicycle path taking extra care there's nothing coming because, in my opinion, cyclists in Hamburg are acutely suicidal.

During my walk I wonder how avoiding the worksite is going to influence my track time, especially after two crucial moments where I was forced to slow down to avoid two idiots going in the wrong direction. Like I said, suicidal, all of them! I finished in 08:42. That was, taking the circumstances into account, not too bad at all.

Wednesday, 26.04.

Today we recorded the second video for my health insurance behind the premises of my work therapist's offices. Again, I had the feeling that the FES wasn't up to scratch. We took off the cuff and made the electrodes dripping wet. All OK after that: Full FES.

Back at home I didn't bother going up to my apartment. I'd already seen that, although dry at the moment, rain was coming. I had about half an hour to do my thing. I grab my iPhone, start the tracker and head off. Time: 08:08. Still getting better! I get the impression that my time for the 200 metres is levelling off at just less than eight minutes. I'll keep an eye on that.

Thursday, 27.04.

Damnation! Stupid me! Yesterday I forgot to plug in the cuff and remote to charge. That was bound to happen at some stage. I was halfway to work when the remote lost its connection to the cuff and sounded the alarm. So I switched it off. But I was clever - having anticipated this - I had the charger with me and charged the cuff and remote at work so that I was ready to walk afterwards.

That's one of the things you learn quickly once disabled: plan ahead! It's the easiest way to optimise your daily routine. And optimisation is very important when you're basically one-handed. It's better to think twice than walk twice. Off to the kitchen? Anything I can take with me? To the bathroom? Washing machine is that way. Those jeans need to be washed soon. Got a free hand? Take the jeans now and you don't have to do it later and if you're already going in that direction, why not do it! It's only little things, but in the end they all add up and save time. After doing this for a while I noticed that the flat is always tidy and clean, everything has its place and I find things quicker. I micro-manage my life. The less time I need to spend on chores, the more time I have to listen to my jazz collection of over 1000 CDs. I'm a big hard bop fan and about a fifth of my collection consists of that genre.

Oh, by the way, my time was slower: 08:35. I had wanted to start walking right after work but my bladder forced me to go up and relieve myself. This gave me the chance of relieving myself not only of liquid waste, but also my big bag. Having lost a load of ballast, I went back down to walk.

It was still windy but not half as cold anymore. Good weather for a stroll. And my walk felt good too. The construction guys had finished their work and the worksites had all been removed and the path cleared. On further consideration, the time isn't all that bad. Not bad enough to feign a depression over.

Friday, 28.04.

That was lucky. I walk my 200 metres; just made it inside before it starts to rain. But, stop! I'm getting ahead of myself. I'm at work therapy, and early, so I use the time and go to the toilet. On my way back to the waiting area Jan comes out with his patient.

"You can go in, I'll be with you in a minute - got something to check in the office."

So I go in and sit down on the treatment table and start the cuff in training mode. My foot lifts and sinks back down every few seconds. Like I always do, I work with my mind and think up and down in accord with the stimulation. I do this in the hope that by thinking with the machine that the impulse stimulates the brain to increase the building of new neural connections in unaffected areas of the brain that then do the work that the damaged areas can't do anymore.

So, the cuff goes buzz: I think <PULL>, my foot rises, no buzz <relax>, foot sinks… Buzz: <PULL> … <Relax>… <PULL> … <relax> and I get the feeling that it helps when I'm involved. I stop helping. The cuff keeps going: foot up, foot down. But not quite as high as when I'm helping. I start helping again <PULL>… <relax> there it is again. Without a doubt, with me helping, my foot rises about an inch higher. It's definitely me. Cool, but I want more. I pause a moment to gather strength. I switch off the Bioness … <PULL> my foot rises … not as high as with the Bioness but it rises about five centimetres, controlled by me for the first time in years. <Relax > … <PULL>and again, repeat, repeat. Every repetition it's a bit weaker.

When Jan finally arrives I can only raise my foot a meagre three centimetres. But that doesn't matter. I've regained some active control of my foot. To celebrate this I'm going to order burgers tonight instead of cooking. At least two, maybe even three. (It was four.)

Oh, I managed the 200 metres in 08:32. Almost identical to yesterday, plus lifting my foot doesn't work all too well at home either. Reason could be the stroll. But I've just been given a major motivation boost. And it's another step in the right direction. Who cares if it's raining?

Saturday, 29.04.

There's a street party on Osterstrasse, which runs parallel to Henriette. So I gotta get outta of this place; fast and far. Such things are way too much bustle and way too dangerous for wobbly people like me. People bowl you over and there's no getting through in a wheelchair. Lucky for me, mum and her partner Michael want to go to Rühlemann's garden market - my preferred place to buy exotic plants. We stow the wheelchair into the car. And I wear the Bioness.

Even though it's a long weekend, nice weather and prime time of the year for gardening the place is still relatively empty at ten o'clock. I start with the wheelchair so that I can do distance, but realise quickly that in the outside areas the ground conditions make wheeling around difficult. When I have to make my way to the toilet, I stand up, leave the wheelchair in a quiet corner and switch the Bioness on. It works fine, even off-road outside. But the place is starting to fill up and when it starts to rain everyone migrates inside. After being nudged a couple of times too often I give up and head for the cafeteria and switch back to the wheelchair - also because it's the only chair left. Mum has her plants together and we're on our way back. She also brought me my new glasses.

Back home I did the 200 metres in 08:38. It was no fun because of the dense hordes of pedestrians leaving the street party. But the weather was good and the trip to the garden market showed that I can do half an hour in difficult terrain. Oh, and my new glasses fit perfectly and I can see with them too!

Sunday, 30.04.

It's perfect weather outside: sky is pristine blue; sun's out; no clouds in sight. Phone says somewhere between 12 and 15°C depending on which weather service you trust. So I go down and outside, but again there's this nasty wind (25 km/h from the southeast. And easterly is, no matter how strong, almost always cold). Pity, otherwise it would have been a perfect day. I have to walk carefully to not get blown away.

Today I have to concentrate on safety and the quality suffers some. Again I use the stick as a brace and lean heavily against it. Safety first in this case - I don't want shattered collar or carpal bones (again). And I make it back in one piece. And 08:23 is acceptable too. Now off to bed for my siesta, because I need to relax - my quad's starting up again.

Monday, 01.05.

I had a look at the physiotherapy videos we recorded and I noticed that overall my gait is definitely getting better but my knee isn't bending at all. In fact it's snapping backward. I'm going to try to remedy that today. I seat myself on my

Theratrainer for just five minutes before I do my walk. Maybe I can activate my knee to bend the right way. It could also be a total flop. I do only two and a half minutes forward, two and a half backwards. It didn't help one bit, no different to yesterday. I only had one wobble because of the wind, and was a little quicker (08:19).

Post-siesta: massive, painful muscle aches in my quadriceps. So it's magnesium again. Knee trial is hereby judged to be an utter failure. I'm not doing that again. But, then again: nothing ventured, nothing gained.

Tuesday, 02.05.

On my way to work I noticed that I keep standing on one leg more often, and not on my right leg, but my left. That I trust my right leg is pretty straightforward. That my body uses my left side so soon after starting use of the Bioness was something I hadn't expected. I'm going to have to ask Artour about that later today ...

Artour noticed that too. He says that through the stimulation my left leg is being put back into focus. And not only the leg, my whole left side is receiving more awareness. Jan from work therapy says the same - that I've made huge steps becoming more conscious of my left side. Through that I've become straighter by trusting that side and burdening it more. I also confessed to my knee trial failure.

"What did you expect? Why don't you let your system get used to it before you start messing around?"

"Yeah, got it, but you know me. When things start looking up, I can't get enough and want more. Sometimes too much."

Anyway today is one of those days with a very high muscle tone, not only my leg but the whole system including arm, neck and especially my hand. Normally I'd take two more muscle relaxants, but that's forbidden, so instead I'll drink two beers later and go to bed early.

After therapy, the weather goes from bad to worse. The heavy clouds have now produced heavy rain. So my walk is cancelled. A pity, but at least I had ten days' steady progress. Maybe I'll squeeze it in tomorrow morning before work therapy.

To pass time, I checked possible upcoming milestones. Next step could be to the Park - which would be 250 metres from home.

Wednesday, 03.04.

I have to get up earlier on Wednesdays. That's because I have work therapy before work. About an hour earlier. That's why I'm still a little sleepy and I'm not going to walk. Jan gives my request for a longer distance an emphatic refusal:

"No, definitely, no! Keep it at 200 for the time being. If you must, you can try deviating routes and different lengths on the weekends. But keep the workdays clean for your report to the health insurance."

Ah, right I almost forgot about them. And again, I was told off for my knee test. We're not going to be able to remedy that knee problem any time soon, so I should concentrate on other stuff like a wide gait and keeping my stick close to my body. Prioritise on balance and posture. No other silly uncoordinated activities.

"Comprende?" - "Si, Señor."

Astonishing! Despite significant fatigue I walked great, kept my left hip (extra) pushed forward and my stick close. Even did a good time: 08:16. Not long and I'll be under eight minutes.

Thursday, 04.05.

Last night I almost toppled. My shoulder collided so hard with the doorpost on the way back to my bedroom, that I very nearly lost balance as I bounced off it. Very close call.

I think the electrodes aren't wet enough because the FES isn't transmitting cleanly. The felt pads are astonishingly absorbent, and look soaked after even a short time under running water, but that's deceptive. Sometimes only the surface is wet leaving the underlying layers dry. As of today I will knead the pads under water and then wring them until not dripping anymore. That should work fine.

This morning I hit another couple of doorposts. This phenomenon started a couple of days ago. And at first I thought it was general clumsiness on my part. But almost falling over last night was an eye-opener for me. Do I put such a load on my left side that I lean over more and hit things or do I feel more and I've been hitting things all the time and haven't noticed? I'll have to ask Artour about that later ...

"No question, a very clear case of left lateral shift. By putting more weight on the left, your centre of gravity also goes left and you're hitting things you would easily have passed in your former askew alignment. You just need to get accustomed to your new situation. Don't worry, it'll pass."

I just hope it doesn't take years. It took me ages to stop hitting things with my right side when I first started walking again after leaving my wheelchair for short distances. After all my last major fall is two, maybe three years back. No wait, more like two.

After physiotherapy, I went for my walk. On my way to the corner it started to drizzle, so I had to hurry up. Under difficult circumstances wearing my hand orthosis and my large bag I cracked the eight minute mark. And it wasn't even a close thing. I did it in 07:16 - a whole minute faster than yesterday.

Friday, 05.05.

Nothing interesting happened today because it was pouring. I even got drenched coming home from work; so no walk. But Jan did confirm Artour's statement to my hitting doors with my left shoulder. I really have become more upright. So that's something. Also, the FES is less distracting. I hardly notice it anymore. Even the erroneous ones whilst standing are now only merely annoying.

Saturday, 06.05.

All morning we had heavy cloud cover. Then, suddenly, sunshine! Quick! But I was too late - the clouds won. However, it was almost warm and the wind was gone. It seems that the clouds have scared everyone away. The streets are empty. Someone in my neighbourhood is having a barbeque, the smell of pork fat on charcoal wafts through the air. Good idea. I should still have some sausages in the fridge. The residents living above me don't like charcoal grills - but my grill uses gas, so that's not a problem. After 07:06, I'm back. Somewhere I must have stepped in some chewing gum. I'm all for a complete ban. Singapore got that one right. Useless, idiotic crap.

Sunday, 07.05.

Today is perfect. We've got clear, blue skies, loads of sunshine, no wind, but (yes, of course there's a "but") for the second time I forgot about plugging the cuff into the charger. Three to four hours charge means I can't go before it's one, maybe two pm. Damn! I lost the morning. Two hours charge might be enough for the short track. In the meantime I chop and marinate veggies for the grill. Take the sausages out of the fridge so they warm up to room temperature.

At one thirty I go downstairs and outside. The first twenty metres I'm almost blinded. I pull my hat down over my eyes - that helps - but walking without seeing properly because of the glare is no fun and I have two wobbly moments. Turns out it's nothing that my newly regained balance can't handle. Back at my starting point I'm a little disappointed. I was hoping for less than seven minutes, but I guess 07:05 is pretty close.

Note:

The next weeks aren't that exciting, and more strenuous, especially for me. It's a bit like in Lord of the Rings, second book, where Frodo and Sam undertake their difficult journey through the swamps of the Dead Marshes on the way to Mordor. It's an astonishingly boring and monotonous read in a book that's otherwise very fluent and has captivating storytelling. I assume that's intentional to underscore the hardships. I admit that occasionally I have skipped pages to get back to Aragorn, Legolas and Gimli's storyline. So I'm not going to be disappointed if my reader does the same. I suggest somewhere in the vicinity of March 17 where there's a surprise. Otherwise, welcome to My Swamp.

Monday, 08.05.

Heavy rain last night - and it wasn't much better in the morning. Closed cloud cover and drizzle. But at noon the clouds dissipated, so after work, I went straight to my track. I made good progress on my way to the corner and raced an older lady with a wheeled walker; and lost. She grinned as she overtook me and pulled away. Today's wind was a poor imitation of yesterday's, but it's still very unpleasant when you get it straight in the face. And again, short of seven minutes: 07:07.

Tuesday, 09.05.

Cramp! And it's a nasty one, at six in the morning. What a great way to start the day. Of course it's the quad again. It's basically the only muscle that's causing any trouble. There are other muscle issues but they don't come anywhere near the intensity of attention that my quadriceps demands. Artour massages it somewhat back into shape. Good enough to try the 200 metres, but it's clear not to expect any record-breaking times with my thigh going haywire. I do a 07:27 which is way better than I expected. Back at the front door I search for my keys ... to no avail. They're gone.

Okay, don't panic. Where did you see them last? Physiotherapy. I call them, they go looking ... nothing! Next in line: taxi! But he's long gone. So I call their hotline.

"Hello, you are a registered customer. If you want to call a taxi to Henriettenstrasse 1 please dial one. If you want to call a taxi to ... <snip> ... If you wish to speak with a member of our staff, please dial zero." I dial zero.

To my surprise somebody picks up immediately. Normally you get at least five minutes of holding loop.

"Hansa Taxi. Hi! My name is...

<sorry, but I forgot your name immediately, so to make things easier, let's just call you Monica>

... Monica. How can I help?"

"Hello Monica, my name is Tim Herzberg and I was just taken home from physiotherapy and I ordered the taxi via app. I think I lost my keys in the taxi."

"App-order by the name Herzberg?" Didn't I just say that? Shouldn't her phone system tell her that? After all, I'm a registered customer. Already a bit on edge, I restrain myself and answer nicely:

"That's right."

"Where did you sit?" Monica asks. This one catches me off guard.

"In the Taxi. A Toyota, one of these hybrid things."

"No, no which seat?" She explains.

"Front left … no, right. Front passenger seat." My left-right problem has, for once, nothing to do with my stroke. I've always had that problem.

"Okay, last question, to where did you go?"

"Henriettenstrasse 1"

"Okay, I'll try to reach the driver. Don't hang up. Whatever happens, stay on the line.

Now I'm curious … There's a beep and the line goes dead… and stays dead … nothing … for about two minutes. Then Monica's back.

"I couldn't reach the driver, but it was Taxi 371. Try calling us again in fifteen minutes and remember: 371."

"371, got it!"

"Right! Bye." And Monica's gone. What next? I could go back to work. I've got a spare key in a drawer there. But I try texting my wife first. She's got a key and works in the near vicinity. And she's online and not in China or the Philippines.

She reassures me that she'll be here as quick as she can. So at least I'll get into my flat today. I take a look down Schulweg and see a mighty familiar looking keychain lying in the dust about two thirds of the way to the Tornquist. Oh, my! I text my wife an all-clear and walk the track for the second time today.

Wednesday, 10.05.

That was the first month and that was quicker than expected. Carolin is joining us at work therapy to check on how I'm doing. And it's always on these days, when time is of the essence, that there's no cab in sight. The app says nine minutes but it's closer to twenty before it comes. I'm going to be late. I warn Jan, but it's okay. We define the next measures. I note that the Standard setup of the FES with five is a bit harsh and I regularly tone it down to four. So we change the default setting. Well not exactly. What Carolin does is shift the intensity of the FES currently assigned to four over to five. (And three to four, two to three and so on) That's because five is always the start setting. So four is the new five.

We didn't have the time to record a new video but we can catch up with that on Friday. We also relieved the quad with Kinesiotape. It seems to work too. Botox is also an option, but only after the three month trial period. Don't want to devalue my test-series.

Very nice: my mother-in-law Renate visited me. She hadn't seen my new flat yet. And we went to a Greek restaurant just round the corner. I walked almost all the way but the path got too steep so I switched to the wheelchair which we had brought along for my return trip. Including that, I walked almost 400 metres. It's a pity that I didn't go all the way, but nonetheless it was a nice extended test for an everyday experience.

All that's missing now is a summary for the first month:

I like it. A Lot! After years of accepting the status quo, I'm moving forward again. It requires a considerable amount of discipline and hard work - things I'm not really renowned for - but as for that, I'm doing pretty good and all the work shows that it's worth the effort, via a number of very amazing preliminary results.. Improved depth perception and regained balance are the most remarkable of the effects. The push in motivation is also unbelievable. The pity is that the after-effect wears off in about half an hour. Without the Bioness my inward rotation is back, my balance is off and there's a general decline in my gait quality. Walking feels wrong without it and it's more tiring, but all I have to do is switch it back on and everything's OK again.

Thursday, 11.05.

I forgot to take my hand orthosis with me to physiotherapy. I always let Artour put it on twice a week so he can monitor what progress my hand is up to. Thus he had to torture me by other means today.

I had a nice stroll, the weather was fine and the 07:15 was okay. The tape on my quad seems to be having an effect - it's way calmer. Dentist: all good, plus the usual: "you should use interdental brushes!"

Friday, 12.05.

Rain. Again. At work therapy we renewed the tape. It really worked. In the late afternoon mum came round and scared away the rain, so we walked together. We should have stopped talking. I didn't concentrate much on time or quality. The time wasn't great - an 08:09. Shouldn't have let it slip. When mum left, the rain came back, followed by a magnificent thunderstorm. Wow. Flash, boom, bang!

Saturday, 13.05.

No idea why, but today is great. I woke up feeling terrific. Well balanced, literally! Felt almost weightless. But, outside, the air is heavy and moist and smells of thunderstorm. I shove the wholemeal spelt bread into the oven and I'm gone. Have to be back before the world comes to an end and the first indicators of that loom almost black over the horizon in the west.

I can't remember the last time I had such an urge to go forward. I had to slow myself so as not to tumble over forward. I had trouble getting my feet moving forward fast enough under my body. But then again - that is exactly what walking is - continuously falling forward and getting your feet back under your torso. The corresponding 06:56 was good too! So was the bread.

Party on the Reeperbahn - and yes, with Bioness still on - but the electrodes are starting to dry and the FES is weakening. I party on until about 1 a.m. when the smoke starts to scratch in my windpipe, and I leave when I start coughing. I just hope that all the smokers don't need a six week induced coma to quit (my "method"). The opiate withdrawal symptoms aren't a laughing matter. Clonidine, Propofol and Sufentanil. Just three of the reasons I'm banned for life from giving even blood plasma.

Sunday, 14.05.

The weather is just perfect. Blue skies and a nice, mild 20°C. Not even a breeze, but the air still retains its morning freshness. It's perfect for a good morning stroll. I doubt that I can crack yesterday's time but the forward urge is still lingering. I start and a few steps into it. Bang! The urge is back with a vengeance. The upper torso wants to move and the rest has trouble keeping up. But today I can control it better, even use it to speed up a little.

I wonder if children have the same feeling when learning to walk and if it's the reason why they topple over all the time. But that's one thing I can't allow to happen. With my 1.85 metres I fall a long way and when my 70 kilos splats on the floor, bones can break and already have: [dislocated fracture of the lt. lateral clavicula 02/2016]. Sometime I also get the feeling that when I'm close to my speed limit my left knee seems to bend a little. Nothing I can control, so I don't worry about that. But I might lower my centre of gravity some more. Who knows? I took another 30 seconds off yesterday's time (06:27). Bring it on!

Monday, 15.05.

The weather seems to boost me. This morning we had closed cloud cover but after work the sun wins and breaks through. But my bladder is under some pressure. Walk ... toilet ... walk ... toilet ... decisions! Am I going to be bothered coming back down for a walk if I head up to the apartment? Come on! Walk! Already on the last quarter I remember: centre of gravity lower, stick closer. Better late than never. But it really is difficult to tell if it's working with the knee. I can't see what's happening. Looking down deflects too much attention away from more important things like balance. My depth perception is getting better but still not capable of delivering that information - yet! So I can only guess about the knee.

Time 06:41. Goal for this week: stay under seven minutes; If possible get under six, but it's okay if I save that for next week.

Tuesday, 16.05.

06:56. And here come the excuses: rain, hand orthosis, big bag, not enough sleep, hungry. Did I mention the rain? Honestly, today is not my day. The day started with an ambulance at five thirty. No, not for me - for someone else - but did the driver have to start the siren directly outside my bedroom window?

Wide awake I got up. Shower, double espresso. I'm early; switch on CNN - amusing: our favourite "apprentice" in the White House has goofed up again. I'm not unhappy that Trump got elected. At least it shows the nutcases on our side of the Atlantic that populism doesn't work.

I take a peek outside, Rain. A lot! Work. Physiotherapy. At least it's only a steady drizzle when I get home. Walk? Hmm ... now that I'm already here, why not? Worst thing that can happen is that I get wet. At least I'm under seven minutes, so the day wasn't a complete waste.

Wednesday, 17.05.

Last night: no ambulance in my bedroom, and today's weather's better too. Forecast: 26°C, but with all the precipitation from the last few days it's going to be really humid, and I have a feeling that my quad doesn't like that.

Today's video shows that I need to concentrate more on pushing my left hip forward. The FES is very distinct, almost painful. I leave work and hit a wall, not literally. I mean the wall of hot, humid air outside. I'm definitely dressed too warm. But the forward urge is back. So: left long ... right shorter. <Repeat> The time is good: 06:20. And I improved my hip displacement.

Thursday, 18.05.

28°C today? I'll believe it when I see it. It's still overcast. Need to go to my neurologist today. My medication is almost gone and I need replacement prescriptions, or I'll run out next week. I still need Levetiracetam: 750 0 750 and Baclofen: 20 0 20 (first number is the morning dose, second midday, last evening. Each in milligrams active ingredient) Levetiracetam is my anti-epileptic, Baclofen my muscle relaxant. Thank god I have no major side effects - and that's uncommon too. Lucky me.

There's more thunderstorms coming. They're not here yet, but I take up a quick pace the first few metres anyway. Something's different. I tire quickly. Halfway there I'm utterly exhausted. The foot drop is back and I keep getting snagged on irregularities in the pavement slabs. Sometimes I get close to falling over. The inward rotation is creeping back too. At first I didn't notice but 60° inwards isn't to be overlooked anymore. What's happening? Yes, the air is heavy. But so was yesterday. Back to the corner of Henriettenstrasse, I check the time: 8:54! WHAT? Close to three minutes slower than yesterday?

Somewhat dejected and tired I trudge back up. In my flat I realise why I had so much trouble today:

I'd accidentally switched the Bioness off!

Usually I wear a coat or jacket of some kind in which I leave the remote of the Bioness. Because of the forecasted heat I didn't wear one today. Instead I stuffed the remote into the front pocket of my jeans. That's where I must have accidentally switched the system off. What astonished me most was how unstable and insecure I am without it and how quickly all my symptoms came back.

At home I switched it back on: foot drop and inward rotation disappear immediately and the bounce is back in my walk. But I am exhausted and my quad is killing me. Apparently he didn't like that either. I can't wait to see if my time tomorrow is back in the vicinity of six and a bit minutes.

Friday, 19.05.

I haven't wet the electrodes enough again and the FES is really weak; nonetheless, I'm still more stable than yesterday afternoon. A little Bioness seems better than no Bioness. I'm going to have to change electrodes before I walk. And to do that, I disappear to the restrooms at work for ten minutes. Now the FES is back in full.

On the way home it starts raining again. Big fat drops but they're only sporadic, scarce. The pavement is only dappled. Shall I risk it? No pain, no gain. Off I go. Worse things than getting wet have happened to me. I make good speed, can keep the stick close. All the negative symptoms from yesterday are gone.

I get away with only about 20 drops on the 200 metre trail and it's a close shave to getting under six minutes. (06:03) Back in my apartment the world outside comes to an untimely end. Those several big drops have brought friends, and they're having a ball.

Saturday, 20.05.

What a night! Haven't experienced a thunderstorm like that since my childhood. No staying long in bed this Saturday. Dad's picking me up around noon for our yearly Herzberg family barbeque. So I've got to walk beforehand.

Out of the shower down onto the track, Brrr. Very cool air this morning. The storm last night has pushed all the warm air somewhere else. But a brisk walk will warm me up too. And the drive is still in my bones.

Despite the cool, almost cold, breeze in my face I make good speed. On my way back the sun comes out to warm me. Back at my starting point I stop the tracker ... and missed the five-something again. I'm with 06:04 - basically the same as yesterday.

Sunday, 21.05.

It's starting to annoy me a little, those four or so seconds. I get up at eleven, explicitly charged both the cuff and remote yesterday so there are no problems. Weather's forecast to be great. For breakfast I eat just an apple, nothing heavy to weigh me down; drink my double espresso.

I put today's electrode in a shallow Tupperware box filled with lightly salted water, weigh it down until it's completely submerged. I even degrease the relevant area of my calf with Sterillium to increase conductivity. Then I complete my ten minutes training until I'm sure the FES is coming through strong and distinct. I give my quad another 10 minutes of contemplative pause to relax. And then I'm off!

Keep the stick close to my body, concentrate on walking correctly. No problems, no need to slow down. Careful, but speedy turn at the corner. Return. Back, I grab my phone, just in time to see the 05:59 change to a 06:00. And stop at the 06:03!

No Joke. That's a bit frustrating - just a little - but it is. What was missing was the weightlessness and drive that I've had the last couple of weeks.

That makes it time to bake brownies. The eggs are a bit small so I'll use ten instead of eight. Now where did I put that half a Kilogram dark chocolate?

Monday, 22.05.

The lightness and spring in my walk are back! I can't wait to get on the track, but first: work.

I have a very bad sagging of morale at eleven and only barely hang onto my composure until I can call it a day. I have difficulty staying awake all through work, but on the track I'm motivated again. After delivering the obligatory third of my brownies to my colleagues, my bag is light again. The high clouds are taking the glare out of the sun. I press start on the tracker, slip my mobile into my back jeans pocket, grab my stick and go for it. I feel my foot roll off correctly over the pavement and push my hip still a little farther forward, a quick but safe pivot on my standard manhole cover on Tornquist.

On my way back there's a tree to the left whose roots have lifted the pavement tiles a little. I always try to avoid that rise and go a little to the right as I pass. But today a pram, two bicycles and me converge simultaneously on the same spot. Me, being the slowest of the four, give way and stand to the left behind the tree and let the others sort it out themselves.

The whole procedure takes less than 20 seconds and I give all I can the rest of the way to make up for that. But, to no avail. Several other pedestrians force me to avoid collisions slowing me down again. Arriving I drop my stick grab my phone and … 06:00.5 NOOOOO! Only short by half a second? You're kidding me?

But at least I now know that it's possible. Without the pram-incident, a sub-six easy!

Tuesday, 23.05.

I brought Artour some brownies and Carolin's business card. He's got a hemi-patient that's probably even more predestined than me for the Bioness.

"Spread the word!" I thought.

After waiting ages for my taxi after last week's Physiotherapy, and the next thunderstorm already on the radar, I decide to walk all the way around the Holsten subway station.

Normally I avoid the punks and drunks loitering around here. And today with still good weather, they're out in droves. But putting caution aside, I start the tracker and I'm off into the fray. Most of them are harmless and polite - but a number of them are so concerned with their own problems that they don't notice oncoming disabled people. I always thank the nice ones that do make way because there's no harm in doing so and hopefully raises their self-esteem somewhat, in knowing that they've done a good deed for the day, by giving way to one in need. Even so, it was like running the gauntlet.

I turn round the corner and the bus blocking the line of sight to the taxistand drives away. No Taxi. Drat - walked for nothing! At least there's still no rain, but it's getting darker. I make my way to the front of the taxistand, stop the tracker and see 260 metres in 06:12 (knowing the inaccuracy of the tracker, I measured it again at home and got a distance of 216 metres). Taking into account I had to fight my way through the crowds, not bad at all.

Even better was at that moment, a cab pulled up. Not one from my preferred taxi company, but since I was paying in cash today it didn't matter. The driver didn't like the destination because the trip was short, but we have something called "Beförderungspflicht" which is an obligation to carry. If I can pay, he has to drive me. Turned out, I didn't have to pull that joker. He pulled into traffic and drove me home in a sour silence. His face lightened up when I gave my usual ten percent tip and rounded up to the next Euro. After that we were friends again, and he even offered to help me get out of the car, which I politely declined explaining (again) that, for me, it's training. He got out anyway explaining that he sits all day and it's always good to stretch his legs a little. Never stop moving. No shit, Sherlock!

I take a peek down my track, still no rain. But it won't stay dry too long. The western sky is almost pitch-black. If I'm quick I might be able to do the 200 metres to Tornquist and back. But how will the already spooled off 210 metres influence that? I've got nothing better to do - so, what the heck!

The scene has a sight Sergio-Leone-western touch. Everyone is fleeing the streets and looking onto the street through closed windows. An eerie silence spreads, (no cars, all the traffic lights are red, the birds have already taken cover from the oncoming thunderstorm.) A lone newspaper page dances to the rhythm of the wind from right to left over the sidewalk. (Left to right would have been more iconic, so would tumbleweeds or a dust devil, but I'm not the one making the calls here). I take my cowboy stance, wide, slightly bent at the knees, squint into the oncoming storm... and draw! ... my phone, start the tracker, and off. And I start off real good. Left hip forward; stick up close. I get into the groove and can even speed up. Quick pivot, and Move.

Then I'm back. Stop the clock and ... 05:59.2 YAY! After a week of close calls I finally did it. Under. Six. Minutes.

Safely back in my apartment, the world outside (once again) comes to an untimely end. Big, fat drops of rain hammer at right angles into the ground. Lightning strikes illuminate the darkness under the dense, swirling clouds. Ten minutes of that and it's over. The sun comes out the birds start chattering again. Thank god that the ground is wet and I recorded the track (I really checked). So I didn't imagine it at all - because it was a bit surreal. ;)

Wednesday, 24.05.

It's way colder today. Off to work therapy. I report the success of the last days to Jan and he had new orders for me:

"Let's try something different. Let's go test your stamina."

"How far I can go?" I ask.

"No, time. How long can you move. Take it slow, easy and keep concentrating on the quality of your gait - that'll be tough enough." He says.

I've been thinking about a shift in paradigm for a while. The 200 metres have become somewhat monotonous and I don't think I'll advance much doing more of that. I've also noticed how tiring is for me. A whole month of "running" is wearing me out. Good for motivation, but it's time to move on, time to set new goals. I think I need a break, so that's it for today; take time to contemplate my new objectives.

Thursday, 25.05.

Seems I needed the break - huge muscle ache - so I get up really slowly. Because I can. Today is Ascension Day, which is one of the scarce public holidays in Hamburg (the Catholic south of Germany has way more - sometimes I wonder how they get anything done.). But, far more importantly, today is also International Towel Day in honour of Douglas Adams.

I take a peek out of the window - a lot of sun - and a lot of wind. So I make my espresso and see, (damn!) the cuff isn't plugged in. I do that right away. It's only eleven so I've got plenty of time. I can walk in the afternoon.

It's early evening when I get to it - about twenty past five. The wind has died down. My first idea was to walk from the corner of Henriettenstrasse to the corner Tornquist and then back and forth until I drop. No, not really - but I wanted to make sure that I'm not too far from home, just in case that happened.

As soon as I got there I felt adventurous and just kept on walking all the way to the park. The incline up into the park was too much for me and after ten metres I turned around. After all, I still had to go back all the distance I'd come. And it was the right decision - back at Tornquist a tremor started to wreak havoc in my quad (something I had to cope with the rest of the way) but I finally made it back in 23:36 and now I'm really hungry (carbohydrates please; and quick!) however, because I took my time, it was quite a nice stroll in the sun and I extended my range to 250 metres.

Nearly within range now is my bank (to replenish my cash) at 300 metres away. Also on the radar is the best fruit and veggie shop in my district – Eimsbüttel. It's 550 metres, but that's uphill all the way - far worse than that little bit in the park - so that's for later. Then again, I don't want to just reach my limit, but extend the limit. And to do that, I have to go past it.

Friday, 26.05.

Today is definitely the nicest day of the year. Sunny, warm breeze, not too hot - just 23°C. Good to go for a stroll, but I've got a lot to carry today. For one: a whole display (six rolls) of Kinesiotape and to top it off, a Bottle of Wild Turkey Rare Breed, Barrel Proof, Kentucky Straight Bourbon Whiskey (I allow myself a really good bottle of quality liquor every quarter year) - so I only went straight to my bank after work and walked home from there. Most of the way was shadowed so I wasn't burnt to a crisp. It was getting really hot.

Because of the heat and the load I took my time and arrived home twenty-two minutes later, with fresh cash in my pocket. Unfortunately, I couldn't take much time to concentrate on gait-quality. With today being the bridging day between yesterday's public holiday and the weekend, almost all of

Hamburg seems to have taken the day off. The sidewalk was packed. I had to be careful.

Saturday, 27.05.

Forecast: 28°C. Having spent a quarter of my life Down Under, I've learnt not to go out into the midday heat, but it works a bit different here in northern Germany. The main heat comes later. More in the early afternoon than late morning. And because of that, (but also because I'm basically a lazy slob) I get up at eleven today. Another reason could be that Natural Born Killers started in the wee hours of last night. Yet another, that the Wild Turkey was pretty good too (well, for a bourbon quite okay, but I like the Bulleit Rye Frontier more). So I'm still a bit sleepy and dawdle through the morning.

All of a sudden it's already one o'clock. Didn't I just say something about noon heat? But my thermometer says only 21°C and the rustling of the leaves in the trees promises a light breeze. About halfway to Tornquist I go back - I forgot my sunnies! Today I definitely need them. The glare from the pavement is intense. So, reset and try again.

Plan for today: off to the park and then try the incline, see what it's got in store for me. But it turns out that's not for me - yet. I get to the park no problem, but then after twenty metres of incline I turn around. Damn, that's steep!

Return trip. Now I've got the sun full on my back of my neck (which triggers thoughts of sunburn), but my left arm got the full dose on the way there and it doesn't even have a hint of red (reminder to self: look for, and if necessary buy, sunscreen) I did the almost 600 metres in 27:39. And I even broke a sweat! (Probably from the heat, not the exertion)

Anyway, I was way better than yesterday. I water my chilli plants before the sun comes round. The thermometer says 25C. Quick! Shut the sun-facing side and open the shadowed side of the apartment. Summer's on its way.

Sunday, 28.05.

That was an adventure of sorts. For one: Summer's here. Two: 600 metres is a long, long, long way. I walked up Henriettenstrasse all the way up to Emilienstrasse. And the sidewalk is totally busted. Just when you think: "Wow! Now that was tricky to handle, it can't possibly get any worse," three metres further along, it does. I mean, I can understand that the sidewalk slopes toward the street so that rain flows to the street and not into the houses on the other side. But does the angle have to flip-flop between zero and twenty degrees at random every two to three metres?

The resulting ruggedness of the terrain is probably terrific training for me. It's definitely challenging. At least someone has a beautiful new path in his garden. On the last third of the way, two of the three rows of concrete slabs are missing completely. All gone, except for the broken ones. They were graciously left behind, making the minefield even more interesting. But one row was there to walk on. Which is wonderful training for someone who's supposed to walk in a narrow line. Thank you for that, whoever you were.

It was 300 metres there and 300 back with a fifteen metre altitude difference. And it took me 22:30. Uphill is hard; downhill sucks bigtime!

Monday, 29.05.

Back to the park today. Depending on which app you ask, the air temperature is anything from 20 to 26°C. Reality will be somewhere in between. The sun's out, but there's some light, high clouds that take the edge off it. The air is humid and heavy, so the cool shade of the park's trees seems very enticing, however, I linger only a short time in the shade because there's not much relief and then head back.

After what I perceived as a three hour stint, I'm back and to my surprise it's only been 32:29 for the 550 metres. But I'm totally exhausted, soaked in sweat. And I hope the weather cools a bit. Count on it: I'm going to bed early today!

Tuesday, 30.05.

I'm a total wreck today. Muscle tone is very high and I didn't sleep well either. At physiotherapy, I let Artour tape my quad. The day's really warm - almost tropical - at least 70% humidity, surely. Don't get me wrong, I'm all for warm, even hot. But please, pretty please, not humid. I like it bone dry like in Australia where 35°C plus days don't affect me as much as 25° hereabouts. That's why I've only done the short-track (06:35). And that's enough for today.

Later: An ice cold, dry, rosé wine in a glass full of ice cubes on my balcony accompanied by some light jazz at sundown. For my taste the wine is a bit too floral - I'm more for the mineral ones. To-do (soon): find a really good Riesling for the summer. Something similar to the 2015 Deep Blue from Tesch.

Wednesday 31.05.

Is it the weather or the longer walks? For the last couple of days I'm exhausted and totally deflated. Pity that the start time of both symptoms coincide. So there's really only one way to find out whether it's weather or distance. I have to ask Jan if I can reduce the distance on the hot days.

Me: "<Whine, whinge, whine>"

"As long as you keep moving, fine. But try to keep up at least the 200 to Tornquist and back." Jan insists.

"That's fair and feasible, will do!"

Whilst recording our next video, Jan notes that my right(!) knee has developed a weird inward rotation. Maybe induced through the reduction of my hip displacement. Great! Yet another thing to counter.

After work, I do the 200 to Tornquist and back in searing heat, but I took my time (10:51), taking care to observe and reduce my new inward rotation, carefully placing each right step correctly. And guess what? It helps. Now all I've got to do is keep that in mind among all the other things. Oh, and one of the two electrodes has given up. No more FES. Dead. I will have to ask Carolin for a replacement next time I see her. Or mail her.

Thursday, 01.06.

Windy! That describes today best. Sunny, but very windy. The shortening of the track has helped somewhat. At the very least my brain isn't as tired anymore. But my body is still not up to it. Sluggish, stiff, muscle-tension - the whole left side, not just my leg.

So I'm going it easy again today. Concentrate more on my gait. I walk around the Holsten subway station after physiotherapy (210 metres in 06:35) - there's less wind there too.

I'm starting to get the hang of it. I now understand more by what Jan means with left step long; right step short. Back home I get a reply-mail from Carolin. She left a new electrode for me at work therapy. Now I have only one problem left: pineapple-ginger-mint-salad or a Malabar fish curry?

Friday, 02.06.

Flashback: the winner turned out to be the curry, but, when everything was finished ... ALARM! My phone warns me "only five minutes to your appointment for professional dental cleaning." Oh, I forgot about that. Thank god my new dentist is in-house.

Turn off the stove, grab my key, off ... Stop! ... Back! Forgot the money. Check if the stove is really off, gargle with a little dash of mouthwash. Out the door and go two floors down. Just on time.

A good hour later my teeth are clean and freshly fluoridated and I go back up. It's only a pity that I have to wait two hours until I'm allowed to eat or drink and I was already really hungry before the dentist. The whole flat smells terrific because of the curry. Its two hours of sheer torture!

Now to what happened today. Work therapy: tape, lots of tape. The weather being (very) nice we went outside for a walk to analyse my right inward rotation. We found out that I concentrate so much on my left leg that I neglect my right and basically just drag it along behind me. So it's time to reactivate it.

Back home, I found that the FES was a little too much, so I lowered it to three. Exhilarated by the right leg revelation, I went for a walk and it paid off. I literally flew down the track and back in unbelievable, record breaking 04:57. Under five minutes. YAY!

Saturday, 03.06.

Thunderstorm, rain, wind, but by about midday the sky clears and the sun comes out. I defeat my inner sluggishness. Put on the cuff, do my ten minutes training mode to activate my calf and then go down and walk.

Today it's going to be the 500 again. I've got a good feeling today, so I exaggerate the flexion (bending) of my right knee to lower my center of gravity again. It seems to help, but probably looks rather silly. I do gather a couple of glances - but I'm used to that - so who cares?

After having confirmed the cliché that disabled people are weird to a small naïve audience, I arrive at the park and go up the incline for about fifty metres and just when it starts to level out a bit, sensibility kicks in and defeats ambition. Don't forget that you still have to go back!

I start my return trip. Back at Tornquist, and thus in well-known surroundings, I remember another task that Jan piled onto me. Straighten up, chin up and look forward to the horizon. Posture! I usually look down as security measure - constantly scanning for obstacles in my path. As soon as I'm past the tree, the way is clear and I try it and look up ... and straight back down again. Oh! Overwhelming insecurity. Okay ... I try it again, and again. It gets better. By the time I'm back I can do about ten seconds, but that sucks! I'm going have to train that insecurity out of my head.

I did the 700 metres in 35 minutes. I even broke a sweat - but once again, definitely more from the 22°C and high humidity. Now all I need is my new bottle of magnesium pills. My quad is already banging on the door.

Sunday, 04.06.

Yesterday's exertion was not without consequences. My base muscle tone is very high and even my ankle is complaining. Astonishingly the quad is pretty calm. Today I'm not going to overdo it. Being Whitsunday, mum surprises me by bringing lunch round. We stuffed ourselves and then tried to walk it off. I walked the 200 metres in 12:08.

Monday, 05.06.

I think I already mentioned that downhill sucks (well, for me anyway…), however, Tornquist is in way better condition than Henriette. Hang on; I'm getting ahead of myself again. Stop! Two, three steps back.

I'm up early to take advantage of the cool morning before the day heats up, so I'm standing ready at my starting corner at ten o'clock. Today I'm going back to the park to see if I can't find a shortcut from the park to Tornquist. That shouldn't be much more than the 700 from yesterday. Map data and satellite imagery aren't conclusive, but promising. There's a side-arm of Tornquist that reaches almost to the park. If I can find a way through there, the park would be easier to reach and the incline not as steep.

So I do Schulweg to the park with no trouble whatsoever and drag myself up the incline to the path that meanders along the northern edge of the park. Instead of finding any way through, there's a three metre high fence preventing my progress. I can even see the end of the side-arm. Damn! No way through. There's a door in the fence, but it's protected by a huge padlock. What now?

I contemplate my situation a few seconds and decide not to go back, but forward. Further toward Emilienstrasse. And then go down Henriette or Tornquist to get back home. There's not much difference in distance and the ground conditions are more important. I decide to take Tornquist down knowing that Henriette is real bad.

I walk all the way to the end of the park and half of Emilienstrasse back to Tornquist, down that back to Schulweg. So, now I'm back in my own territory, I actually enjoy walking the last 100 metres and it's there that I realise how tightly I'm clutching the handle of my stick. White knuckled. That's going to be a problem tomorrow - all the way up into my shoulders - when the knots in my muscles uncramp. I loosen my grip and the tension eases a little. Speedily, I pass the tree and the rest is easy enough, except for the light tremor on the last twenty metres.

In whole, I walked 1.08 kilometres in fifty minutes. I'm grilling tonight to reward myself and I get the feeling that I'm going to be able to sleep real good tonight.

Tuesday, 06.06.

As expected, I slept really well, but I woke up feeling like I'd been run over by a steamroller; mashed to a pulp. Despite this, after work I did the 200 metres to Tornquist in under six minutes (05:50) and there's nothing more to report for today. Siesta!

Wednesday, 07.06.

Better, but still far from good. Mostly muscle ache. Weirdly my triceps - right arm - too. Probably remaining from clutching the stick too hard.

At work therapy, Carolin came over and we aligned our strategies for reaching my long-term provisioning of the L300 and how to deal with my health insurance. The system isn't only expensive but literally unknown to them and the decision is bound to go all the way up through their complete hierarchy, making the hurdles greater than they already are.

We have to kick off the process soon. Wednesday next week marks two thirds done. Carolin will initiate the negotiations shortly, with the aim of preventing gaps where I would have no system, so as to avoid provoking negative effects. We also taped my shoulder to bend it back into shape.

Meanwhile outside: heavy rain, lightning, thunder. Great! It's been pouring all morning. After work and back home, there's a small gap in the clouds over Hamburg and I risk it. After all, it's not cold, just uncomfortable. My walk is unproblematic. I can even concentrate on the details. On my way back I get a nasty headwind blasting the drizzle straight into my face. It's more uncomfortable than expected. And I finish the standard 200 metres in a disappointing 06:30. I don't get too wet, so throw the moist clothes into my dryer, rub my face and hair with a towel and all's good.

Thursday, 08.06

Only my upper back and quad are tense. All other aches and pains are gone, but there's still this continuous heavy drizzle and more of this stupid wind. Not good conditions for a walk - and I was game for a stroll to the park today.

I wait a while and it gets better. At least the rain is almost gone, but it's only 15°C. Judging by the experience of the last weeks, the wind is only nasty on my way to Tornquist. On the way back it can even propel me a little. However, it's disgusting when the drizzle blows directly in my face - and that's exactly the way it is when I get moving.

My glasses are instantly speckled with tiny drops of water impairing my sight, making it difficult to keep my mind on my inward rotation and keeping my left hip forward. But as soon as I reach the corner and turn around, it's only half as bad. Again, I forget to over-ride habit and lift my head up and look forward, so it's only on the last fifty metres that I glance up and forward every now and then as safety allows. In spite of all the difficulties, I manage the distance to the park and back in 24:43.

Friday, 09.06.

The air is heavy again, warm, very moist, choppy winds. All my senses say:" Warning! Thunderstorms are coming." Weather radar says I've got about an hour before it hits Hamburg, and it's going to be a big-time storm. I decide to do a speed-run. Just the 200 metres today. After starting, it takes a couple of seconds to get into the groove. Yes, walking for speed was only a couple of days ago, but it seems I've gotten used to the long-distance walks quickly.

No matter. I keep going, building up speed, but the drive doesn't kick in. I compensate for that with improved technique and that works for a while, but the occasional gust of wind knocks me off my concentration. Two thirds of the way back a small tremor hits my leg. Oh? Still recuperating from my kilometre? I guess a week isn't enough. But throwing myself to the floor and chucking a tantrum isn't an option. There are dark clouds looming in the west. Time to move! The clock says 05:21 when I arrive, which isn't too bad.

A salad later, and well into my siesta, a BOOM rips my sleep apart. Lightning must have struck somewhere really close by. The storm is here. I open a window as it starts to pour out of the heavens. I close my eyes and gently doze back to sleep, to the soothing white noise of the torrential rain.

Saturday, 10.06.

I should have realised it earlier - all the signs were there in plain sight. The wind is gone and the air is heavy. The sun has evaporated all the moisture that came down yesterday. The tracker is running and so am I. There's lot's happening on the sidewalk.

Mostly kids running about - which makes me go even more carefully - but as we know, I'm not running for speed.

People pull up with their cars, unloading trunks full of big plastic boxes stuffed with toys. All of them heading for the park. Baggage carts pull past me. Parents herding their lively kids are all over the place. People have to get off bikes to avoid hitting them. It's getting worse and worse. (I've got nothing against children when they come in pairs or even triplets, but when they come in larger herds, chaos reigns). And it's too much for me. I still don't have a clue what's up but I now realise that something is going on. Could it be? Is it? I get to the park, turn the corner, and my worst nightmare becomes reality. A huge children's flea market in full commotion.

I turn around as fast as my feet allow and strive to put distance between it and me. Flea markets are dangerous enough. People all keep looking at the offered goods - not looking out for passing disabled people. I used to love flea markets but now they are just a steeple chase with potentially deadly obstacles. Having too many close calls of almost being pushed over, I tend to avoid them now - even more so if they're full of kids mucking about.

When I get close to home a tremor slips in through the defences to annoy me for the remaining thirty metres. At least I was exposed to the sun for 24:02. I grill my four remaining Merguez and call it a day.

Sunday, 11.06.

Nine thirty a.m. and already back? What happened? Well, for one, forecast for today says 29°C. So, it's walking either very early or very late. And then waking up at seven a.m., why not early? It's good that I bought sun lotion because at just past nine, the sun's already going flat out.

Lather with sun cream liberally, wide brimmed hat, shades, keys, phone ...Off I go! Not much happening early Sunday morning, the streets are still empty. A few people crossing Schulweg with bags of breakfast buns from the bakery across the street dodging the even fewer cars on the road. Some people that are seriously into sport are already underway. Runners (not joggers) pass me occasionally. A peloton of five, six cyclists fly past me in formation.

The quietness of the morning lets me concentrate on the quality of my gait and a good part of the distance I can look towards the horizon. I can even do a little extra into the park parallel to Schulweg by staying in the shade, extending the 500 by about 150 metres.

Back at Tornquist, which I was about to cross, I stop when a car slows down and indicates that it wants to turn into the street. Enter unknown man, stage right. He jumps between me and the car onto the road. Gesturing the driver to stop and let me through first. At this point, I'm not even on the road - still a good metre from even the curb. I explain to the unknown man that the car is probably faster than me and I've got all the time in the world, and that it was a nice gesture but totally unnecessary. Together we wave the bewildered driver past.

"But I was only trying to help." He explains, obviously disappointed. I thank him again, and go about my way.

This happens often. People that don't have much contact with the disabled are often unsure about how to react to, and even interact with, us. Some things are simply unnecessary. You don't have to run across the room to open the door for me. If you're not there I'd have to do it by myself anyway. I had to (re-) educate the smokers loitering around the ashtray on the park deck at the back entrance of my employer's office block. At first they almost fought over who would have the honour of opening the door for me. Until I said, "No! Stop - that's training for me. I have to do it myself, so everyday life gets easier to cope with."

Astonished, they backed off and let me do it myself. And see, I can. No problem. I mean, it's only a door. Isn't it? It's okay to keep holding the door open until I've passed. I do that for others too, but only if you're going through yourself. That's simple courtesy and perfectly fine. Going out of your way to do it, especially for me, is in a way degrading, even insulting. If I really need help, I'll ask.

"Can I help?"

"Oh yes, I need to borrow your time machine, mine's broken. So I can go back to 2009 to tell myself that there's a time bomb tickin' in my head ... And I'll even give it back to you last week."

"????!??"

"No? But thanks anyway, I'm doing fine. Everything's under control. It's all just training. From nothing comes nothing."

In the meantime, I'm back home and happy that the day started with a brisk stroll of 31:40 in the cool of the morning. Only the light tremor on the last 100 metres impairs the overall picture. My thermometer already says 23°C. I drink buttermilk mixed with banana juice for breakfast and start into the Sunday.

Monday, 12.06.

He's back!

My good old buddy, Mr. Muscle Ache.

"Hi there, I was expecting you. But it was rather cheeky of you to bring your whole family with you."

"What do you mean? You invited all of us yesterday yourself. There's even a recording I could show you."

"I did? That's not how I interpret it, but now that you're here I can only do the short-track today. I want you all out the door by tomorrow."

And I doubt they'll heed my request too.

Today started sunny, then all of a sudden someone switched the lights off - dimmed it down to ten percent. Dark clouds pass overhead. Gusts of sharp wind blow first this way, then that. Drizzle!

After work, I take my time preparing my salad. Simply burning time, then out of the blue: Sunshine! Rain and wind gone. My time is 14:40. Nothing earth shattering, but the dark clouds coming in from the west could be. And, of course, they catch up with me. The downpour gets intense but I'm almost back. I get hit by about 20 major-league drops, but my hat catches most of them. The entrance to my apartment building is roofed so I don't get any wetter as I look for my key. Behind me the world comes to a temporary end. I turn round and contemplate the end of all things for a moment as lightning starts to tear the sky to pieces. I go inside, turning my back on Ragnarok. I hope my salad hasn't wilted too much.

Tuesday, 13.06.

Today is going to be another of these hauling jobs. I need to take about two kilos of the finest direct-trade coffee beans home. Direct trade is even better than fair-trade. Several small roasters across Europe have joined forces and each deal directly with small coffee farmers in Africa and Central America. Dealing fair contracts for small batches of ecologically sound beans. If you really like a particular bean then you'd better buy more quick because the amount is limited and next season could taste totally different. Diversity rules! The coffee isn't cheap but the proceeds go directly to the farms and their workers and not to large industrial roasters that dictate unfair coffee prices and only offer medium quality beans. You can even check each contract with every single farmer online. Now that's transparency for you - and they taste way better too. Anyway, my espresso machine demands a refill, and my big bag is completely full of beans.

Yesterday, I started considering how to tackle the logistics of this event and how to intertwine it into my training. Do I run all the way up and leave the bag in my flat before I run? Do the short track with the load? I could park the bag under my wheelchair which sits in a quiet corner of the entrance hall, but that would mean leaving my money and the precious coffee alone - who would be so malicious as to steal a bag under a wheelchair (even if it is full of first-grade coffee that smells real great)? Also I'll only be gone for a quarter hour. Decisions, decisions. It's not even clear if I can walk. While at work the weather's still nasty, but today I've even brought a jacket along.

Which in the end, I needed too. The bag was so stuffed with coffee it didn't fit under the wheelchair. I just put it on top. The steady rain had switched to a light drizzle. Whilst walking I could even take time to counter my still exist right inward rotation. And this time I don't forget about looking forward, but in a drizzle that's no fun.

Some fifty metres to go, the drizzle switches back to steady rain. With twenty to go, steady becomes heavy and I get seriously wet on the rest of the distance. Without hat and jacket I would have been drenched. Back home, I fumble out my phone with clammy fingers and stop the time at 15:27. My beans are still there. I trudge upstairs to dry. And a fresh espresso.

Wednesday, 14.06.

Second month over; eight quick weeks. Time for another summary.

The longer walks are hard on me. My quad especially doesn't like that, but only afterwards. Whilst I'm walking, all is fine; then as soon as I stop, he kicks right on in. Could be a question of more training.

But the positives are even better. I hardly notice the FES any more, even whilst standing. It's become routine. But the effect is still there: foot drop and inward rotation are still countered. There are still days when I'm more sensitive and feel the buzz again, but then I just tune it down a little. On the majority of days I feel close to nothing. I even have days where I have to increase up to six because I'm having a numb day.

Astonishing is how quick the symptoms come back without the stimulation. An almost instant return to foot drop where I start catching edges in the sidewalk again, my balance gets worse and I have to lean on my stick more. With the Bioness I can walk a kilometre. Without, a hundred metres were just barely possible, if that. And if that's not a reason that speaks for the system I don't know what is. Yes, there are side effects, (that damn quad and the occasional tremor), but the positive effects outweigh the negative by at least a mile.

Today, I feel a few of the negatives. A light tremor on my way back and my ankle is pushing its way to center stage. So I take my time and do a slow 30:18. But no matter - the weather's fantastic and I wanted to go outside. That's another positive. The quality of everyday-life and my range have taken a giant leap forward. Even after two months of hard work I'm still surprisingly motivated.

I've grown much more aware of, and have greatly improved, balance and posture - although both still need more work. I still have to remember to straighten up, hold my head high, tip my hip forward and so on. Seven years as a sack of potatoes can't be remedied in a matter of weeks!

The left lateral shift has become normal again as Artour said it would. I stopped hitting things about a week ago. By far, most importantly, I've learned to trust my left leg again. I put a lot more weight onto it, which improves the sense for my centre of gravity I'm still not at 50:50 but 60:40 is way better than my usual 90:10 ratio. I doing so I can reduce pressure on the stick which in turn eases the strain on my right arm and shoulders.

I've even lost some weight. Keep it coming!

Tomorrow's forecast is a whopping 29°C and evening thunderstorms. Who would have guessed? I'm keen on them sticking to the "evening" part, so they don't get in the way of the plan I've got for tomorrow. More on that later. As for now, I'm a little tipsy. Who would have thought the two IPA (India Pale Ale) craft beers would have hit home that hard. So I brush my teeth and I'm off to bed.

Thursday, 15.06.

Today I was out and about for one and a half hours, but I confess: I only walked 35:59 of it. Let me explain: 25°C, no wind and a new idea. Yes, thunderstorms anticipated in the early evening, but that seems to be the theme of this summer - cool, windy, light rain OR warm, windy, thunderstorms. Sometimes you lose, sometimes the others you win.

So I grab my bag, put in my Kindle, which I've charged overnight. Off to the park for a nice afternoon of reading a book. The stroll was uneventful except for the young woman who decided to pass me, cutting my walk and then blocking the whole path with her bike to take her time to cover herself with sunscreen at right angles to, and in the middle of, the footpath. I had to skirt around her, blocking the path for two other riders who saw that I didn't have a choice. I just shrugged my shoulders and shook my head in dismay. They understood, their faces full of contempt for the woman lathering up.

That's another good example of a base problem with our current society. This after-me-comes-nothing-but-myself-mentality. Sometimes I get the feeling that nowadays most people have real physical pain by thinking any more than a short distance ahead, of other people, or maybe even thinking at all. That would explain a lot. Best to stop thinking altogether. Don't get me wrong, I'm not expecting more empathy or courtesy towards me in particular, just a little more in general would do this world a great deed. Several seconds later, she overtakes me again – this time without stopping. By then I've almost reached the park. I walk up the incline scanning the area for a bench in the shade. None to be found - at least none that aren't already occupied.

I'm already about a third through the park when I spy one on the other side of the park, across the meadow. So I do the dangerous thing and go for an off-road walk across the uneven ground to the other side hoping that he bench is still free when I get there; also hoping that I don't topple over in the middle of the meadow with no way to pull myself up again. I don't, and as a bonus it's still free.

After slumping down on the bench I pause the tracker, and start reading "Leviathan Wakes" from James S. A. Corey. I've been looking for ages for a new sci-fi novel to start on, so I checked the winners of the Hugo Awards. I picked the winner of 2011.

Let's see if I like his style. Lost deep in the asteroid belt somewhere between Jupiter and Mars, I realise it's getting colder; the sun's gone. No, not literally. The sun can't just disappear. It'll still be there, it's just clouds that have pushed themselves between it and myself. And the wind's picked up, becoming gusty. Are the thunderstorms early? Why risk it? Off home I go.

I disentangle myself from the strap of my bag; a young woman asks if she can help me. It seems there is still hope for our society after all. I smile and thank her but I have to do it myself, you know, training. I check my watch. A good hour. Not bad at all. I unpause the tracker and get down to the tedious task of getting home. Still pondering the story it's back at Tornquist by the time I remember the things I have to train and I concentrate on quality on the last 100 metres. Better late than never. 700 metres overall - and I like the story, although it seems familiar.

Friday, 16.06.

After a quick bit of research I found out why the story seemed so familiar. Netflix is making a series out of it called "The Expanse", and the first season was great, loved it, but now I'm in a dilemma. Stop reading and wait for season two, or read on and spoil the series? Probably be easiest to find something new to read.

The weather's weird today. Sun, torrential rain. Sun, rain, sun again. A switch every ten to fifteen minutes. A quick check on the weather radar shows what's up. A large system of small thunderstorms is moving across northern Germany from west to east. Let's see which side will show its face when it's time to walk … It's the sunny side, but the next storm's already looming dark in the west.

With no time to waste I get moving. It's time for a speed-walk again. 05:26 is the result - and not a second to spare. I just made it inside. The outlook for the weekend is better. At least it's supposed to be dry. If I find a new book in time I might even do some more reading in the park.

Saturday, 17.06.

Sometimes it just doesn't work out. It all looked quite innocent. Dry, very sunny but a sharp wind. I step from Henriette onto Schulweg and I'm almost blown away, literally. I wasn't expecting that. And to top it off the wind is icy too. I go back up in search of a suitable coat. I check the weather situation online. The wind has turned from westerly to north-north-westerly overnight. That's exactly the orientation of Schulweg, turning it into a wind tunnel. 20km/h winds may not sound like much, but when you're on one and a half legs, it's enough to become a serious hazard. I go anyway. I'm no quitter. But I'm only doing the short-track. It's supposed to be 20°C but that figure doesn't take the wind-chill into consideration and that's definitely a factor today. And it's a fight - especially on my way to Tornquist. My stick's doing overtime with the wind in my back. Compensating for the gusts is hard work. The way back is easier, but by no means easy. Going in that direction I can lean into the wind, which makes buffering the gusts easier. No chance on working on quality. This was 15:47 minutes of tough workout. Can't wait to see what tomorrow has in store for me. The good thing about negative experiences is that they highlight the positives. What would the stars be without the darkness between them?

Sunday, 18.06.

Today I woke up aching from top to bottom. Muscle ache; high base muscle tone. Lower back in knots. But aside from the physical ailment, psychologically, I'm not even half arsed. Regular down in the dumps. Yes, that happens to me too. Rarely, but it does. What's up? Yesterday's wind? Cumulative fatigue? Who knows; who cares? So I make my espresso, down my pills (I take an extra Baclofen - don't tell anyone) and chew some pieces of ginseng root. I started with this last winter, for an increase in energy and motivation. It gives a generally more positive disposition to everyday life. Sometimes that helps and so there's no harm in that - and if I ever needed that, it's today. Or possibly, I'm going to skip my walk. Maybe, after fifty days of hard work it's time for a break. But I'm in no rush. It's Sunday. I keep breakfast simple. Buttermilk mixed with fresh orange juice. That's it.

At about ten o'clock I see that, once again, the cuff hasn't been charging overnight. Yes, I forgot it. Again! I plug it in now. Now I've got three to four hours of forced wait ahead of me. So I make a quick lunch: ravioli with a mushroom, lime and sage sauce. The buttermilk breakfast wasn't too filling. The ravioli are filling and I they force me into a siesta afterwards. I'm gone in a matter of seconds. I have a really good sleep and wake up totally refreshed. The battery's full. Not only mine, but the cuff's too. Even the grey clouds have broken apart and there are patches of blue peeking through. So it's time to move some. Tracker on and Go!

I wanted to take it easy today, but as soon as I get moving I hit the right groove and it's not only easy but quick too. I pick up speed as I go along and the drive kicks right back in, all the way to the park and back. And I only need 19:36 which is great and under twenty minutes. Time for more magnesium.

Monday, 19.06.

07:19 on the short-track today, because it's really nasty outside: 27°C and very humid. Possibly the only reason to avoid the tropics. But when you think about it, the medical care there is also pretty basic. And the therapy is probably not up to scratch either. Health insurance? How's the neurologist density. Upon further reflection, it seems there are a lot of reasons against the tropics. Dengue fever? Several types of Meningitis, Hepatitis, Malaria? Leprosy? I get it. I'm staying in Hamburg. Who needs beautiful beaches? Palms don't cast too much shadow anyway.

Because of the heavy tropical conditions I've slowed down and concentrate on gait quality, which works great. I can't wait for my ice cold Coke that's waiting at home for me. Coke says Drink at 3°C in their ads. I like it a little colder so I've set my fridge to 2°C. See - I'm a rebel.

Tuesday 20.06.

Really nice weather. Still pretty humid but only 20°C, and a nice cool breeze. Perfect for a walk. Artour's just put my hand orthosis on, but that's no hindrance, or so I thought. However, when I get to Tornquist things are feeling wrong - probably my orthosis - and I increase the impulse intensity from five to six. When I get to the park the inward rotation is back and getting worse by the minute. I decide not to go into the park as planned but turn for home instead.

Back at Tornquist things are going haywire. The inward rotation is somewhere between 50-60°, my toes are grinding over the pavement, catching irregularities and I really have to watch out so as not to trip over. It's like the time I had accidentally switched it off. The LEDs on the remote were lit when I increased the impulse to six so it should be on. Is something wrong with the cuff? I can't check it whilst walking so for the remaining hundred metres I take real care and go very slowly so I don't trip or make things worse. When I get to the shade of the front door I'm totally spent, I can rest a little and lean against the wall, and I can now take a quick look at the remote.

The remote has four buttons. Two to regulate the intensity - one for up, one for down. Then there's the ON switch. When pressed it switches on the remote and searches for the cuff on its 2.4 GHz band and negotiates the connection. Once the connection is established it blinks green. The last button switches the cuff on which then blinks yellow. And that's the one I didn't press after leaving therapy. Damn! You can change the intensity without having the cuff on - which is what I did on my way to the park. I just missed that the button wasn't flashing yellow. I switch it on and, as if by magic, with the very next step, everything's OK again. I roll off over my foot correctly again, inward rotation gone. My time is so disastrous I'm not putting it to paper. But I did do the 500 metres without the Bioness. Where's my Coke?

Wednesday, 21.06.

Today was crap! Don't get me wrong; my time was OK for the long tour (not the very long one - just to the park and back), and getting to the park wasn't a problem, but on the way back when I was almost at

Tornquist, I got hit by a major tremor. So I slowed down. Just past Tornquist my quad cramps big time. Under pain I hobble back to my flat in 19:14. Who knows what an unbelievable time I would have done had all gone well. Seems that yesterday's experience is still lingering to haunt me. Time to lie down and maybe take an extra Baclofen. I'm all done with today.

Thursday, 22.06.

Thank god for coffee. Without it, there'd be no reason to get up. I haven't slept too well and the quad is still complaining. My base muscle tone is, well, let's say it's been worse. But not by much.

When I'm done with work, a huge storm front hits northern Germany. Almost all major airports shut down; all flights delayed, cancelled or redirected to southern airports. Rain so heavy that I've never seen anything like it - and I'm the sort of guy that stands on our protective dikes pitting himself against storms with winds higher than 9 Bft. I can't do that anymore, and I miss it. I love being exposed to the elements, but even I take cover when half-inch hail comes down as it does today. And then all of a sudden it's over and the sun comes out. The hail on the street is ankle deep but melts quickly - after all, it's supposed to be summer and we've got at least 20°C.

To calm my quad I only do 200 metres (6:37) and hope that my leg gets better. This evening Artour told me to tone it down a bit. And I second that notion.

Friday, 23.06.

"Are you sure you know where you're going?"

I look up from my feet and see a young man getting off his bike in my direction with concern written all over his face.

"Sure do." I reply. Concern changes to scepticism.

It takes a couple of seconds for me to realise what's happened. I'm on my walk and had just finished my careful pivot on the sidewalk to Tornquist. A tall skinny man with a stick does an abrupt, clumsy U-turn for no apparent reason? He must think I'm confused, if not disturbed, maybe even mentally deranged. Escaped from a psychiatric ward? Drugs? Better not get too close. Might be dangerous. Does he bite? Zombie-alarm! I explain it to him:

"Don't worry. I'm fully oriented, just not too good on my feet. I'm doing my daily training and here is where I turn."

We both continue on in different directions. I finish in 11:36. Why so slow? It seems that I'm still struggling due to the 500 metre session without the Bioness. I still haven't quite recuperated from that and I'm still a bit wobbly. That's also the reason for my careful turn. I thought the short-track would be a good re-entry point. Maybe I was wrong. Jan, like

Artour, said I should slow down for a while. I should try using my Theratrainer again - but only arms and shoulders. To tell you the truth, I'm looking forward to a break.

Saturday, 24.06.

I'm not doing anything today. First: it's pouring outside. Second: after two months of full throttle I've earned myself a couple of days off.

Sunday, 25.06.

Today I did a little more. I did some arm training with the Theratrainer ten minutes clockwise, seven and a half counter-clockwise. Why seven and a half? Well, it seems that my hand is currently so supple that, despite being fastened by Velcro and a neoprene glove my hand kept slipping off the handle. Not being able to control my fingers and therefore not being able to grip the handle by myself I have to affix it to the handles which then go round and round taking my hand, arm and shoulders with it. After slipping off the seventh time I was fed up and broke off the session. I'm going to have to look for the rest of the Theratrainer accessories. If I remember correctly there was more bondage stuff in the bag.

The quad was doing better, that was until I took down the garbage with the Bioness on. I should have refrained from going three times. Once would have been enough. The first was the normal trash which needed to be taken down quickly. On these warm days, bacterial colonies quickly evolve to civilisations capable of space travel, but I could have left the other three bags of paper waste for the cleaning lady on Tuesday. Of course I didn't - and now my quad is hard again. Not as bad as a couple of days ago, but bad enough. At least the garbage is gone.

Monday, 26.06.

Still pausing. The garbage run was a real setback - but I didn't completely go without training. I wore my hand orthosis for my whole workday. I might start running again tomorrow.

Tuesday, 27.06.

The weather fits, the rest doesn't. Sleep was unsatisfactory, muscle tone is very high and to top it off I seem to have caught myself a cold. My nose is dripping and I have the feeling I can sense every blood vessel in my head pulsing to the beating of my heart. I went to work anyway, and I call my Physiotherapy studio to ask if they want me. They don't! I can understand that. They have to be picky about that sort of stuff. Therapists do house calls for bedridden patients. The spreading of germs and viruses is careless if not dangerous. So after work, I go straight home and straight off to bed. I'm not in the mood for walking.

Wednesday, 28.06.

Way better today. My nose has stopped dripping and the throbbing in my head is tolerable. I take two Aspirin and decide to do at least the short-track today. I take it easy and only do a 13:49. The exercise did me a world of good. I realise that I even missed it. A bit. The quad however, didn't - but he has to get used to it, 'cos I'm not going stop rolling yet, as I've noticed when I don't keep moving, the days start to blur into each other. Somehow you get caught in a suspended state of indifference. And that's frightening.

Thursday, 29.06.

Warm, heavy air! 25°C and very humid! Sunny too, so it's going to get worse. Thunderstorms are expected in the early evening. My definition of summer differs somewhat - but no one asked me - so we take it as it comes.

Artour strapped my arm to the orthosis. It's getting warmer and warmer which does comply with my understanding of summer. If only it weren't so damn humid. I start to doubt that I'm going to go for a walk.

And if it weren't for the breeze coming up to intervene in the heat, I wouldn't have walked, but would instead have gone straight to my Coke. Thanks to the light wind I did a smooth 11:16. And my quad's doing better too.

Friday, 30.06.

It's pouring rain. Yesterday Berlin drowned. A foot of water standing on main roads and being our capital city, its drainage system is pretty much up to scratch. Not as good as Hamburg's as we do get flooding regularly and are somewhat prepared. Our city is criss-crossed by waterways that merge into the river Elbe. Nonetheless, there's a reason I bought a flat on the second floor: global warming, sea levels rising and the like. On my way home I got the hit by the rest of a normal shower and the start of a bit of very heavy one. So I only got wet and not drenched. Bonus.

Saturday, 01.07.

Like I said drowning Hamburg isn't going to happen soon. And it didn't, despite the torrential rains last night, which kept raining till late morning. Afterwards I do get to walk. Walking is tough today so I go slow and concentrate on quality - after all it's the weekend - and I do a 10:42. Up to now, this summer has only got potential to get better.

Sunday, 02.07.

Guess what? When I get to Tornquist it's drizzling again. I thought I'd go to the park today. Somewhat discouraged, I turn around because it's getting dark again and it's only 2 o'clock. Just past midday.

Good that I did too. When I get back it's a steady downpour and we've only got 14°C. I don't get too wet - thanks to my coat and hat - which I had grabbed because it was overcast all morning. My time was good with 06:21 - only because I had a weather-induced driver.

Hey! Would someone shout at the responsible guys up top: we've got summer down here! Or at least we're supposed to have it.

Monday, 03.07.

Someone heard me? Lots of sun; almost no wind. Nice and warm. Was it that hard? The quad likes it too. So it's 500 metres again today. I'll have to be quick about it. Yes, thunderstorms this afternoon - again - but for now it stays nice, even gets a little better.

So does my stroll. Just the last hundred metres are tougher. Goes to show how quickly your stamina dissipates if you don't keep it up doing distance training. And I swallowed an extra Baclofen this evening - I know I shouldn't - but we've already taken the step to start negotiating with my health insurance. They've already got a copy of my report, so the time is not of importance anymore for them: 22:06.

Tuesday, 04.07.

Under six minutes again. And I didn't even need the drive I needed the last times. It might have been because I did it the wrong way round. How's that? Let me explain: I woke up early. I opened the door to my balcony and a cool breeze washed around me. I thought to myself:

"Why not walk in the cool of the morning instead of the noon heat (if it happens not to rain, thunderstorm, hail or whatever), and do that before work. It's not as if I get all sweaty from the exertion. Is it?" I can at least try.

There's a lot going on. It's mostly commuters on bikes; scattered pedestrians thrown in here and there.

I'm lucky in this regard in two aspects. For one: my metabolism was always really high to begin with, so I really never did have problems holding my weight. Second: now through my high muscle tone I burn a lot just standing. Because the muscles in my left side are constantly doing overtime, I burn a lot of calories without me doing any extra sport. I stay between seventy and seventy-five kilos depending on the amount of sweets and chocolate I eat. A small tip on the side: the easiest vinaigrette is Mustard oil,

Honey, vinegar, a little salt. Shake until emulsified. Done. Be careful not to use the massage mustard oil, get the edible one. The other can be for external use only. My walk was very good and despite the heavy traffic I kept a close eye on quality. Also there's no reason to for any extra muscle relaxant because I've just taken my regular dose. But the best thing is: I've got a free afternoon.

Wednesday, 05.07.

What a screwed up day. Again, I wanted to walk before work, but then I remembered that Carolin wanted to meet Jan and me at work therapy. We have to discuss further measures because the medical service of my health insurance (MDK) has turned down the videos we took to prove the improvements I've made over the weeks. Excuse: I'm wearing jeans so they can't see my knees. Are they serious? That, of course, is just a pretext. They're just preparing their case against the system. After all it's not cheap. But what good things are? I'm already seeing myself walking around behind the work therapy offices in only my jocks. So I'd better not exhaust myself beforehand.

So walking before work is called off. As usual, my cab takes ages to come to me. At the end of the week we've got the G20-summit in Hamburg, and most of the taxi drivers have taken the week off. Taxis are scarce. Again, I'm late. But at least I did come. Carolin didn't. She's sick. But Jan and I did make new videos. Thankfully indoors; with and without the Bioness; from two different angles.

The difference is definitely visible. Even for a novice like me. Jan will write his report in the next days and I will write a short one page personal statement. We're not going to hand them this text because it's too long and not factual enough. Instead, I've written a short version parallel to this one, stating only the facts, which we sent to them a couple of weeks ago. It seems that the clerk responsible for me is already convinced. Only the MDK is the final hurdle.

I order my groceries online and have them delivered. I do this about once a week and today it's time again. My salad reserves are almost depleted. I have to stock up. The delivery time window for today is between three and five p.m. usually they deliver in time. Not so today. At least they called me to say that it'll be later. It was almost six o'clock when they finally arrive and my desire to walk is almost diminished, but I went anyway and I did a quick 06:26. I did notice a large increase in police presence whilst walking. At least seven patrol cars pass me on the short track and one police van has taken position on the verge of the park - probably to deter illegal campers.

In the meantime my porkölt is simmering away on the stove. Porkölt is what we Germans call goulash. Goulash is a soup in Hungary, not a meat stew, and since I'm cooking a stew it's definitely a porkölt. My secret ingredients: real pork lard, lots of marjoram and charcoaled skinned red bell peppers. After three hours in the pressure cooker it's so delicious I eat way too much. Owww! my belly.

Thursday, 06.07.

Today I walk before I work! The police presence has toned down a little. Only four patrol cars. And the park isn't under siege anymore. I do the short-track in 06:41. And for a change the quad isn't mucking around at all. Off to work!

But the way back was a real adventure. The G20 summit really thwarted my plans. Hamburg's senate's guest house where Trump is staying (All major hotels in Hamburg declined to take him) isn't even a kilometre away from where I work and when White House apprentice arrives, all streets within this kilometre are shut down. Completely! Had I left only twenty minutes earlier, I would have been safe and sound in a taxi and been out of here. But now, no avail. Police everywhere and traffic jammed as far as the eye can see.

The taxi app says the next taxi is only eight minutes away. I order, but no one answers my request. On my app I can also see where free taxis are and the next taxi stand where two are waiting is only 500 metres away: all the way down the Hans-Henny-Jahnn-Weg.

After waiting ten minutes I give up waiting, and start walking to the taxistand. The sidewalk is nice and level but full of people idling about. After all, the weather's nice and warm and sunny, and it is a rather touristy area I work in. I reach the Mühlenkamp where the taxis are supposed to be. But they aren't anymore. What now? The roads are jammed here too; the cars not moving an inch in any direction.

In front of a restaurant, I find a place to sit and ponder my situation. I could just wait. But it's only about two o'clock. And it's going to take hours for the traffic situation to ease. I could just walk across Sierichstrasse - that's always been a natural boundary of sorts.

To explain this I have to go way back. This is the story a taxi driver told me: Back at the end of World War When Hamburg was and occupied by English forces, their garrison was not in the middle of town but to the north. The personnel carriers had to move soldiers from their base to town centre every morning and back every evening. To reduce traffic jams, some upper echelon decided to make Sierichstrasse the axis of this operation and commanded that the driving direction for both lanes of the street from midnight to midday was into the city and for midday to midnight it was out from the city center. And it's been like that ever since then. Unique in Europe, and much to the liking of commuters, and to the surprise of foreigners who turn into it in the wrong direction at the wrong time of day. Because of that, the traffic situation on the other side can be totally different. Or so I hope.

It's really nice outside and I'm game, so off I go, staying in populated areas in case I need help. I walk down Mühlenkamp towards Pölchaukamp. And what luck, on the corner there's a taxi stuck in traffic. I ask if he's free.

" Yes, but we're all trapped here, all exits are blocked." He says.

" Mind if I just sit down a bit and see how it goes?" I ask.

"No harm in that" he agrees. And I get in. After ten minutes and about fifty metres in the wrong direction I realise we're not going anywhere fast. I'm quicker if I walk by a long shot. And I've only got €30 cash on me. I ask if it's OK if I get out again.

"Be my guest," he says. "Today's screwed anyway."

I get out and walk back to Pölchaukamp in two minutes. Way quicker! I turn left walk to Sierichstrasse (which is empty - at two o'clock, direction is out of the city and it goes directly past Trump's abode where it's certainly been closed down). But the jam goes across Sierich and I follow it along Fernsicht - still jammed but now only into the city. (Out is free. That's a good sign.) On the Ktugkoppel-bridge I spot a free taxi going in the wrong direction. It's the third taxi I pass but this one is without a passenger.

"Wouldn't you rather go to Eimsbüttel? In the direction you're heading there's no movement at all." I ask and explain.

"That's where I' coming from since…"<he checks his watch>"… about four hours ago. I've reached my revenue target for today and just want to go home." Later I heard that some people were stuck for up to seven hours.

I wish him good luck and move along. Places to go . people to see. Astonishingly, I'm doing fine. No tremor or the like, even the quad is nice and quiet. After the bridge there's a park to the right and I spy a free bench in the shade. Why not take a break? Who knows how long this is going to take. No harm in that.

At the next pedestrian crossing I switch to the other side of the road and head for the bench. I sit down, relieved and somewhat proud at what I've managed to achieve. For safety reasons, I've been in contact with my wife Mattea over the last half hour, (if you're forced to do potentially dangerous trips its better someone knows where you are) just in case I collapse. She's on her way to me by bike, so I don't have to walk alone for the rest of the way. I send her my coordinates. I also told her my plan was to walk to Mittelweg, maybe Hochallee, where I'm sure the roads are free again, but for now I enjoy my break in the shade with a very nice view of the outer Alster. I also see that the battery of my phone is running low. So I kill all the running apps, which is a mistake because I also kill the tracker which is monitoring my progress. I'm going to have to re-measure the distance at home. But that's not really a problem.

Hellwigstraße
Leinpfad
Möven
straße
Andreasstraße
Wentzelstraße
Bellevue
Rondeelkanal
Gellertstraße
Fernsicht
Frauenthal
Hellwigstraße
Bobby
Reich
Mittelweg
Eichenpark
Scheffel
Harvestehuder Weg
Krugkoppel
Bellevue
Alsterkamp
Alster
Harvestehuder Weg
Hamburg-Nord
Eimsbüttel
Sophienterrasse
Mittelweg
Harvestehuder Stieg
Harvestehuder Weg
Willhelm-
Gymnasium
Mittelweg
Pöseldorfer Weg
Harvestehude
Klosterstieg
Uhlenhorst
Uhlenhorst
Alsterchaussee
Fahrdamm
Alsterchaussee
Rotherbaum
Alstervorland
Alster
Böhmersweg
Pöseldorfer Weg
Pöseldorf
Brodersweg
Mittelweg
Magdalenenst
Milchstraße
Harvestehuder Weg
Bei St. Johannis
Milchstraße
Mittelweg
©OpenStreetMap-contributors
N

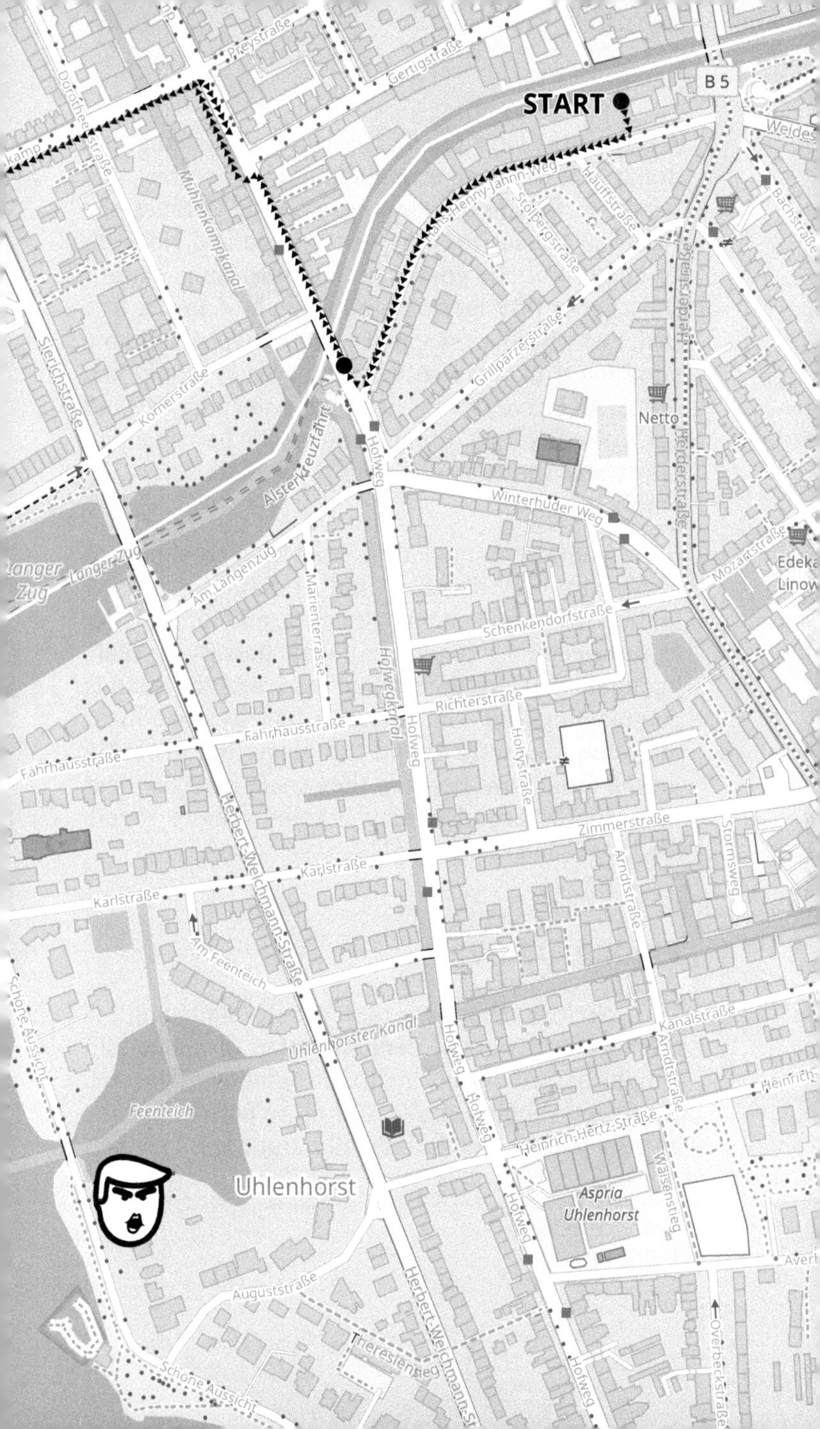

START
B 5
Weides
Bachstraße
Preystraße
Gertigstraße
Dorotheenstraße
kamp
Mühlenkampkanal
Hans-Henny-Jahnn-Weg
Stolbergstraße
Hauffstraße
Grillparzerstraße
Netto
Sierichstraße
Kornerstraße
Alsterkreuzfahrt
Hofweg
Winterhuder Weg
Mozartstraße
Edeka
Linow
Langer Zug
Langer Zug
Am Langenzug
Marienterrasse
Schenkendorfstraße
Hofwegkanal
Hofweg
Richterstraße
Holtystraße
Fährhausstraße
Fährhausstraße
Herbert-Weichmann-Straße
Zimmerstraße
Arndtstraße
Stormsweg
Karlstraße
Karlstraße
Am Feenteich
Kanalstraße
Schöne Aussicht
Uhlenhorster Kanal
Hofweg
Heinrich
Feenteich
Heinrich-Hertz-Straße
Waisenstieg
Uhlenhorst
Aspria
Uhlenhorst
Aver
Hofweg
Auguststraße
Herbert-Weichmann-Straße
Overbeckstraße
Schöne Aussicht
Theresienweg
Hofweg

A short time later Mattea arrives. I tell her that I'm doing fine and we can head off right now. She proposes to ride up some way ahead to check the situation ahead from my perspective and rides off to do so. But she comes back almost immediately. Only about fifty metres up ahead she found a free taxi, which she stopped. After explaining my situation it is now waiting there, ready to take me home. All I have to do is get up this steep incline and get in. Before I do, I thank Mattea for her time and effort and she rides off. And the streets are really empty.

Back home, I immediately boot my notebook to remeasure the distance and come up with 2.5 kilometres in two and a half hours; and for that, I'm astonished that I'm not completely destroyed. Yeah, I can feel that I've done some work and the quad is complaining, but I'm not even half as done-in as after the kilometre round the block. It'll probably hit me tomorrow. I reckon they could have the next G20 somewhere else. Maybe some remote island. Ah, there's my Coke. Gulp!

Friday, 07.07.

The circling choppers are really annoying. A moment ago a small demonstration of about 200 people passed by my bedroom window. Peaceful, young folks followed by six or more patrol cars. It's all very non-violent. But not all Hamburg is like that.

Only two kilometres away in the Altona district, cars are burning - two of them police cars.

Not sure if I'm going for a walk. Despite yesterday, I'm feeling up to it. But first my double espresso. No work today. We've all been given the day off. There's no getting there for me anyway. My taxi app says the next taxi s a good forty-five minutes away. Half the streets are closed off again, and I doubt that many taxis are underway. Online you can live-track the demonstration - there are none headed in my direction. The electrodes are wet and positioned on my calf. I refrain from wearing one of my black hoodies (it's too warm for one anyway) and I grab a colourful hat and hit the streets. Every now and then a light tremor, the quad is doing overtime.

A car backing out of a garage blocks my way. The boot is full of beach stuff, air-mattresses, towels and the like. I'm not fleeing the city for the beach. I just want Tornquist and back. The tremor intensifies but doesn't hinder me from walking. Three choppers are still circling above Sternschanze - the protest's hot-spot. Four police vans rush past me, lights flashing, followed by a swarm of patrol cars, sirens wailing. Back at the door, I stop the tracker at 06:53. Not bad considering yesterday's ordeal.

Saturday, 08.07.

Weather's fantastic. And after a heated night the riots are over too. The stone-throwing criminals (I can't and won't call them protesters because they're not - if you throw a stone with the intent to hurt someone you're no protester) gave up immediately after the police sent in heavily armoured SWAT units and they came down peacefully from the scaffolding after seeing that they were up against assault rifles. Thank god that our weapon restrictions are in place.

It would have been a bloodbath had the rioters had automatic weapons instead of bottles. This morning there were more taxis underway in my district of Eimsbüttel than patrol cars. Things are calming down.

A final joint statement: WE all agree - except Trump. He's leaving the Paris climate agreement. It's Trump vs. the rest of the world.

Here's a joke about that:

Earth and Mars come closer to each other again after millennia of riding along their respective trajectories.

"Hey Earth! Oh, you look terrible! What's happened to you?" Mars asks.

"Yeah, I know. I feel terrible too; I think I've caught myself a bad case of Humanity." Earth replies.

"Ah, okay, I had that once, a long time ago. Don't worry it'll pass ..."

It was a short night again because of the circling choppers. Getting up out of bed was arduous. I walked all the way to the park. The way back was extremely strenuous and to top it off, I forgot to start the tracker so there's no time to report. A very unsatisfactory morning.

Note: Turkey's Erdogan won't let his parliament ratify the Paris Agreement either. Add Putin and that officially makes them officially a Clique (might be something for Assad too). Now they can start a self-help group for populists. Trump has still a lot to learn from them on oppressing free media, opposition, NGOs and other nuisances that impair real power.

Sunday 09.07.

Today I've got a time: 30:17. Not that good, but I was distracted. In the vicinity of Tornquist on my way to the park: Police sirens in the distance. Then over speaker:

"ACHTUNG! STEP AWAY FROM THE STREET, CONVOY COMING THROUGH!"<repeat>

First, two police motorcycles speeding ahead to the next intersection, blocking the crossing traffic. Followed by two patrol cars, three large black limousines with black windows, two black vans, and three more patrol cars. Finally followed by two more motorcycles speeding past the convoy headed for the next main intersection. Sadly, the limousines didn't carry flags so there's no way of knowing who was being hurried to the airport. But at least I did get a bit of G20 flair at the end.

Last night there were riots in the Sternschanze again, but this time the police were quicker in encircling the so-called Black Block, and dividing them into easier to handle, smaller groups. But there were still burning cars.

Sometimes I just don't understand some people. If you live in such a hotspot, why park there if you know that there's rioting going on or even if there's rioting anticipated? That's just plain stupid. Park your car in an outer district and ride in by train. No pity from me if your car goes up in flames.

To tell the truth, cars go up in flames every now and then anyway. A couple of years ago a gang of rich kids were arrested for torching cars. They did it because they were bored.

Last night was very warm and sleep was impossible due to the aforementioned choppers. I opened my bedroom window wide to let in some cool night air. It faces Schulweg - making it virtually impossible to open because of the intense noise the traffic provides - but tonight is very calm because of the high police presence due to the rioting.

Only people that really need to be out are up and about. Patrol cars or police vans speed past in one or the other direction, lights flashing. The occasional stray taxi does too, mostly away from the action. I can see three choppers circling over the "Schanze" as we call it. It's only just over a kilometre away as the crow (or in this case chopper) flies. There's still no red glow on the horizon from that direction so I'm not worried. I also have NTV on, which is showing live what's going on. Only a few barricades have been torched so there's no immediate danger.

Then, at about two a.m.: Two medium sized dark limousines with Hamburg license plates pull up in front of my window and park on the side of the road (blocking two garages I might add). Four large men get out, dressed in dark, casual attire. They build a loose group on the sidewalk, turn to and start looking in direction of the Schanze into the dark. A few minutes later, as one adjusts the plug in his ear, which I hadn't noticed before, and starts talking into his collar in a muffled voice, I get it. Two unmarked police cars and an undercover unit have taken position as scouts. Waiting for stray rioters that have escaped the police circle around the Schanze. Exciting! I go to the kitchen grab a chair and two beers. After all it's a lovely warm summer night. I enjoy the cool breeze and my beers and go to bed. Two of the choppers go away and the noise becomes bearable. The undercover unit was still there when I turned in at about four o'clock. And like I said, the night was short.

Monday, 10.07.

Afternoon; I should have walked in the morning. It was dry then. It isn't anymore. Dark clouds push across the city. It's supposed to get better later, but it doesn't. More rain, rain, heavy rain. Yuck!

Tuesday, 11.07.

Tomorrow the three-month test is over. I would have liked a more fitting, even spectacular, ending to my trial period. But, as so often this summer, thunderstorms ... again. And with them come gusty winds. But I'm not here for fun - I wait for a dry patch - and I'm off!

I start like the other 74 times from the corner of Schulweg/Henriettenstrasse and take off in direction of Tornquiststrasse. Thanks to the thunderstorm my plan to take a break on a park bench is foiled, so I pay meticulous attention to the quality of my gait. No rush on my last official walk.

I keep my stick close, roll off over the whole foot, left hip forward, left step long and far to the left, nice and wide. Right step not quite as long, but also wide.

Most of it has become routine. My hip displacement has become dramatically better. My drop-foot is gone, the inward rotation too - at least it is when the L300 is on.

I'm much more upright, my posture has improved. I use my left leg as far as possible, putting weight on it again. My balance isn't yet where I want it, and I still need my stick, but I'm on my way to reducing pressure on the stick as much as is safe.

I can still feel the 2.5 kilometres from last Thursday in my bones, but I did manage it quite well. And I'm pretty sure that I would even have made it to the Hochallee by myself if necessary.

Coming from a range of barely fifty, and on good days, maybe a hundred metres, I now do at least two hundred on a daily basis. More than often, even 500 metres - and that without having any major problems. All in all, that's pretty unbelievable.

OK, the trial is over. I've done my best; all I can; and, on occasion, even more than that. Now it's up to my health insurance to judge if the costs are worth the improvements. I've hammered the ball to their side of the court with all my might. Now it's their turn. I've heard that my personal clerk is already convinced. It's only the MDK that has to be swayed.

Oh yeah, the last official time was a casual 11:29.

Epilogue

MPM and Carolin have guaranteed that they're not going to take the system away from me until they really need it. So I can keep using the rent unit for a while longer. I might have to pay rent at a reduced rate though, if my insurance takes too much time. I can understand that. Can't have resources wasted.

Tuesday, 08.08.

Today I woke up with a stiff neck. Last week I bought two new pillows for my bed, which I still have to get used to. I'm sick and tired of waking up with back problems. Now I'm working my way through Ikea's collection of pillows. I still need to find a new use for the huge Cuban flag that was my pillow before.

I didn't walk before work today because I stretched my lie-in time to the max, so time was short when I finally got up. I needed that today.

Well into work, my phone rings and I see that it's Carolin. Oh no, bad news? My health insurance has probably declined the Bioness system and we now have to formulate an official protest.

Me: "Hi Carolin."

"Hi Tim. How are you?"

"Fine, up to now," I answer cautiously.

"Well, you're going to be much better now. Your Bioness has been approved!"

"Seriously? So the Physiotherapists report was the decisive factor?" I reply.

I'd asked for reports from my neurologist and physiotherapists ahead of schedule just in case the insurance company declines my request. Already having experienced denials involving my Theratrainer and foldable wheelchair and knowing the procedure involving the formal protest and following proof and report chain; this time I intended to be prepared.

My physiotherapist had already written his report and I'd forwarded it to Carolin. We were waiting for the report from my neurologist to send them both to the MDK, when I found out that my doctor had gone away for a three-week holiday. Not wanting to waste time, Carolin had forwarded the physiotherapy report on Monday to the MDK.

"It wouldn't surprise me taking the timing into account. But there's no way to tell. You know how well the MDK is shielded."

That's true. Carolin, Mattea and I had all tried to reach the responsible person in the MDK to ask if there's anything we could do, but to no avail. We were all stopped and reprimanded before we got through to him (although we had name and phone number). It seems all external incoming calls are fished out to a help desk that filters and blocks inquiries of any kind.

"But that all doesn't matter anymore. Because I've got the oral confirmation and will probably have written one on my table by tomorrow. When I do, I will order your very own L300 unit." Carolin says.

"That's great. Thanks. Hope to see you soon, when we swap systems," I reply.

Well that was not what I expected! At best I was expecting a decline requiring my formal protest. I don't think we would have landed in court. My case is too clear for that. It seems that it was clear-cut enough not to be declined in the first instance. I seem to be biased by bad experience.

Thursday, 10.08

Today I did walk before work, but I only did the 200 metre short-track because I was a little late. Time: 06:03 - short of sub-six minutes again, but not by much! But it doesn't really matter. I've got nothing to prove anymore.

At work my phone rings. What now? All my people chat nowadays. The actual act of making an actual phone call is reserved for emergencies - or at least only for very important messages. Ah, but no. It's Carolin again. Damn, No written confirmation? Has someone made a big mistake, all back to zero?

I open with: "Hi Carolin."

"Hello Tim. Guess what I've got lying in front of me right now?"

" You're kidding me. That quick?"

" Yeah, I've got a brand new L300 waiting here for you. When can you pick it up?"

 "Well, I've got work therapy next door tomorrow, how does quarter past two sound? But I've got to check with Jan if he wants to be there too - then we can do the hand-over after, or instead of, therapy. I think I'm his last patient so I think he could have spare time."

"It'll be more a trade than a hand-over - I'd need the rental unit back."

"No problem. What's with the old electrodes? Are there new ones included?"

"I think there are. Just bring everything along and we'll sort it out when you get here. If possible, I don't want to use up Jan's free time - after all - it's his weekend. Take that into account when you speak to him."

"Here's what we'll do. We'll meet at MPM at 14:15; Jan can come if he wants to. The switch shouldn't take too long and with the rest of the time Jan and I can go back and do whatever therapy we still can. How's that?"

"Great! See you tomorrow."

Wow that was quick. How cool is that! I get my L300 tomorrow.

I just hope that I find all the accessories from the rental unit. Don't forget the charging cables.

And yes, that was important enough to call me.

Friday, 11.08

I think I've found it all. And most of it fits into the case. I just couldn't remember where the charger sits. So I stuffed it next to the cuff. Not pretty, but I can close the lid without anything being jammed or under pressure. I've even charged it overnight so the next user can start right off. Pull the zipper closed and stuff it into my big bag. Off to work.

Funny feeling without the cuff around my calf and the unusual instability is shocking, so is the drop foot and inward rotation, which are back too. I've decided not to wear the rental cuff today, just to feel how it is without. I haven't done that in months. And yes, I'm too lazy to unpack it all again - but it's more to see how necessary the system is. A final test just for me.

I get there half an hour early. Because my bladder is full I go to work therapy because I know the toilets there; it's always easier if you're in a rush. I can also catch Jan and more importantly, he can carry the case (which is getting rather heavy).

Jan has still got someone in therapy. Like I said I'm early, so I take a seat in the waiting area. I pick up a copy of my first book. They usually have a copy or two lying about. I flick through it finding three mistakes. I put it away again and turn to the Washington Post on my phone. The dispute Trump vs. North Korea is heating up. Not funny.

At this moment the door to the treatment room opens. Jan and his patient come out. It's time to go. As we walk over Jan reprimands me to walk more upright. I tell him that the Bioness isn't around my leg, but in the case he's carrying. I'm already doing my best.

We arrive and I wave to the receptionists.

"Hi, me again. Appointment with Carolin at 14:15, room three?"

"Hey, more posture please. You can do better than that."

Jan shows them the case and explains the situation that I'm not wearing the system.

"We're here to pick up Tim's unit."

We go upstairs and into room three. Not too much later Carolin arrives carrying one case. My case! She disappears for a moment to wet a new electrode (the old ones land in the bin). Meanwhile, I drop my pants. I put on the cuff while Carolin loads my setup from the patient database onto the new remote and she's glad that she doesn't have to explain it to the patient today. Pants back up and ... drum roll ...test walk. I stand up, switch it on and all the dreariness and heaviness that have been following me all day are blown away. Even the drive is back.

I walk a couple of rounds and Jan is awestruck by the difference. It's the first time he gets a direct live comparison. Carolin and I do a few minor adjustments. And then I try it without weight on my stick. I do two, three steps, a little wobbly, but no "Woahhh" this time. Not real good, but not too bad either. Way better than four months ago. It's still going in the right direction.

We then debate my knee and what to do with my inability bend it. My job for the next month is to get a Botox consultation in the University Clinic in Eppendorf to dampen the intensity of my quad so we can then try the L300 PLUS- system on me which stimulates quad and hamstring and might give some control back to the knee. Jan will search for off the shelf static orthoses that inhibit the knee from going the wrong way. He thinks that they will probably force my system to collapse completely, but I'm not sure; we'll see. Let's do some experimental tests. I'm game. As long as things keep moving in the right direction you can count on me.

Then everything is said and done, we're finished. Mine! For as long as I need it. I thank Carolin, and we'll keep in touch, and she said something about regular maintenance checks. We go back down again and back to the receptionists:

"Unbelievable! The difference is astonishing. Your gait is miles better."

Mattea picks me up. We wanted to go shopping and then dinner, but I'm totally exhausted from the day without the cuff and we decide to postpone the party. I'm going to call it a day and go home. But tomorrow it's back to two hundred metres, minimum. If it's not raining. After all, it's summer. Sort of.

Disclaimer:

All in this text occurring technical and medical descriptions, ideas, and opinions are highly assumptive and speculative and come from a totally deranged and heavily brain damaged mind and should not be taken too seriously and definitely not literally!

Special thanks

Jan, and the entire squad of Ergoteam Ottensen.

Artour, and the Achilles Altona team.

Carolin, and all of Mittelpunkt Mensch.

 Dr. Rosenfeld, my neurologist.

Mr. Kraus, from my health insurance.

Mattea, Renate, Elsa, Michael, Jessica and Stefanie for putting up with all the updates, sometimes on a daily basis.

Bioness, for the NESS L300®,

Christoph, Ross, Gesa and A.J. for editing.

And all those involved that I forgot.